COMHAIRLE CHONTAE ÁTHA CLIATH THEAS
SOUTH DUBLIN COUNTY LIBRARIES

LUCAN LIBRARY
TO RENEW ANY ITEM TEL:

Items should be returned on or before the last date below. Fines, as displayed in the Library, will be charged on overdue items.

23. APR

28. JUN 01

1997

ISSN No. 0332-4893
ISBN No. 0 947897 18 6

©
Published by
THE ECONOMIC AND SOCIAL HISTORY SOCIETY OF IRELAND

CONTENTS

To
Margaret MacCurtain

I

INTRODUCTION

The revival of feminism in recent decades has brought an upsurge of interest in the question of women and work. In 1972 the *Report of the Commission on the Status of Women* suggested that wider employment opportunities and entitlement to equal pay were essential steps in improving the status of Irishwomen. Yet concern with women's employment is not new. In the 1830s the POOR INQUIRY IRELAND COMMISSION collected data on the earnings of women and children, which they regarded as essential contributions to the income of labouring families. Attitudes towards women's income-earning activities varied, depending on where the work was carried out, the type of work performed and whether it conformed with stereotypes of femininity. Most eighteenth-century descriptions of women working as spinners in their homes are generally positive; they emphasise the valuable contribution of women's earnings to the family economy. In contrast later descriptions of women's factory employment, or of women working at home in 'sweated' industries, tend to emphasise low rates of pay, poor working conditions and the neglect of children and house-keeping duties. Women's work has rarely been viewed merely as a source of income; it has tended to be evaluated in the context of women's wider roles as mother and carer for the family. As a result, there is more information available on occupations which appeared to conflict with women's domestic role, such as factory employment, than on more 'appropriate' activities such as women's work on the family farm. This preoccupation with women's factory work has often led people to believe, incorrectly, that women's work began with the industrial revolution.

Part of the confusion results from the difficulty in defining the concept of 'work'. The definition used by TILLY & SCOTT: 'productive activity for household use or for exchange' excludes 'strictly domestic activity—child care, cooking, housekeeping'—unless performed by paid servants, but includes food preparation

1

or textile and garment making for the household.[1] Many women might object to housework being excluded. The Cambridge economist A.C. Pigou pointed out that the national income fell when a man married his housekeeper! Recent estimates suggest that the economic value of unpaid housework (almost all performed by women) amounted to 25-40 per cent of the Irish Gross Domestic Product.[2] The occupational tables in the Population Census provide another set of definitions. Until the Irish Free State census of 1926 introduced the category 'engaged in 'home duties', which is not found in the Northern Ireland Census, women without specific occupations were counted as 'indefinite and non-productive' along with children and others without jobs. Farmers' wives were not counted as part of the agricultural labour force except in the 1871 Census, though the 1927 Irish Free State Census of Agriculture, which included part-time workers, indicated that over 263,000 women were engaged in agriculture, compared with a figure of less than 109,000 in the 1926 Population Census. According to the 1979/80 Farm Structures Survey, over 145,000 women were engaged in agriculture, 94,000 of them farmers' wives; the Population Census only counted 12,671. Farmers' daughters and other female relatives other than wives who worked on the family farm were not counted in the agricultural labour force until 1926. Female relatives of farmers were not the only group of women to be ignored by the Census of Population. In 1871, the only occasion when the number of wives working in family businesses was counted, there were 11,020 shoemakers' wives, 2,899 wives of butchers and 3,829 wives of innkeepers. In 1933 the Irish Free State Census of Distribution counted 61,615 women engaged in retail and wholesale businesses, compared to 43,594 in the 1926 Population Census; given that only 82 per cent of retail businesses provided returns to the Census of Distribution, the true number of women working in distribution may have exceeded 70,000; most of the workers not counted by the Population Census were assisting relatives.[3] HIGGS has shown that many women who earned regular wages were returned as unoccupied in British Population Censuses during the late nineteenth century; this may also have happened in Ireland.

The practice of under reporting women's work predates the official census: only 20 per cent of widows enumerated in a 1799 census of Carrick-on-Suir were recorded as holding identifiable occupations, but CLARKSON & CRAWFORD have concluded that many of these 'unoccupied' women were 'probably engaged in the manufacture of woollen cloth as unpaid family workers or employees of clothiers'.[4] Women's employment has tended to be under-recorded because they often combined working in farming or in industry with family duties. In 1812 WAKEFIELD praised domestic spinning as ideal women's work on the grounds 'that it can be suspended and resumed without any inconvenience and thus small intervals of time are filled up that would otherwise be lost'.[5] Census forms made no provision for workers with more than one occupation or those with part-time jobs. While these are important factors, the tendency to assign women to the domestic or unoccupied class reflects society's belief that this was their appropriate place.

In the modern world we tend to distinguish between paid and unpaid work; in the past this dividing line was less clear-cut. Many women worked within the family economy where payment for finished products went to the head of the household, who was generally a man. Family need rather than individual choice determined whether women worked within the family economy or outside the home. If the family could not provide work, young women and men went into service; often their wages were paid directly to their father. Although most women's earnings supplemented the family income, they appear to have had some discretionary control over the money which they earned. According to WELD women spinners in Co. Roscommon spent part of their earnings on 'ornamented clothing' and were generally up-to-date with 'modern fashions'.[6] Income from the sale of eggs was traditionally regarded as belonging to the farmer's wife (BOURKE 1993). The long-term shift in employment from the family economy to the wage economy offered potentially greater independence to working women, though this should not be exaggerated. Most wage-earning women in the nineteenth century were poorly paid and worked out of necessity; the potential independence offered by paid employment only came with higher incomes and was first realised by educated women in white-collar or professional occupations.

Many of the factors which influenced the pattern of women's occupations in Ireland were common to other western economies. The range of tasks carried out was remarkably similar in most countries. Women generally worked in service, the manufacture of textiles and clothing and at specific agricultural tasks such as dairying. On the whole their jobs were regarded as less skilled; few wére apprenticed and while women were often regarded as unsuitable for jobs which required physical strength, many women working in coal mining or farming carried back-breaking loads. The reasons why women's work had a generally lower status are too complex for us to explore here: the explanation lies in society's attitude towards women and involves relationships within the family, property rights and women's reproductive role.

The changes which have taken place in Irish women's employment over the past two hundred years also reflect the changing structure of the Irish economy: the rise and decline of the domestic textile industry; industrialisation in the north-east; falling agricultural employment; and the rise of a modern service economy, which meant that tasks such as nursing or preparing meals were increasingly carried out outside the home. The story of Irish women's employment from the Famine until at least the 1960s must also be placed in the context of falling total employment, late marriages, high marital fertility, a high level of permanent celibacy and a significant level of emigration. By 1911 one quarter of women aged 45-54 had never married, double the figure in 1841; for those who married the age of marriage rose from 24 on the eve of the Famine to 28 by 1911 (Ó GRÁDA, p. 215; KENNEDY & CLARKSON p. 167). For Irishwomen declining marriage prospects (marriage being the most common 'career' open to women) appear to have coincided with a reduction in opportunities for paid employment. It is therefore scarcely surprising that by the end of the nineteenth century single women seeking paid employment, or perhaps a husband, accounted for a majority of Irish emigrants (FITZPATRICK 1984, p. 10). High levels of permanent celibacy and emigration persisted after Independence. There was a strong current of opinion in Irish society that, where possible, jobs should be filled by men (who were assumed to be supporting a family), or by widows and single women with dependants, rather than by married women and single women working for 'pin-money'. The dominant ideology of independent Ireland, which placed considerable emphasis on women's domestic role, has often been held responsible for the low proportion of women in the labour market; in fact these attitudes may have been a response to conditions in the labour market (DALY 1995).

It is impossible to determine precisely what changes have taken place in the number and proportion of women who have been employed over the past two hundred years. In eighteenth-century Ireland, irrespective of how work is defined, all members of peasant households and of labouring or artisan households probably contributed to the family economy if they were capable of doing so. Productivity was low due to lack of capital, and consequently incomes were low. Most households could not survive on one man's earnings. In extreme cases where families were desperate and there was no employment available, women and children took to begging (CULLEN 1989). If there was no work available in the household, boys and girls often became servants (the term at this stage denotes a live-in employee who might work in agriculture, a trade or housekeeping), so that they were not a liability to the family (DICKSON 1991). Most women in eighteenth-century Ireland made a substantial contribution to family income, in cash or in kind. This was less a matter of choice than of necessity and the type of work was dictated by family circumstances and by the opportunities available rather than by a woman's wishes. Women had less bargaining power than men and as the Irish population rose they may have found it more difficult to find work.

The available figures on women's labour-market participation, taken from the Population Census, are presented in Table I. They suggest a long-term pattern of declining employment, which persisted in the Irish Republic until 1981. In that year women accounted for a smaller proportion of the labour force than in the late nineteenth century. However, aggregate data conceal important changes in the nature of women's employment, such as

Table 1.

Number of Women with Designated Occupations 1841-1991#

	IRELAND	IRISH REPUBLIC	N IRELAND
1841	1,169.5		
1851	938.2		
1861	845.7		
1871	817,3		
1881	814.6		
1891	641.4		
1901	549.9		
1911	430.1	267.2	162.9
1926	520.6	340.2 (257.6)*	180.4
1936	—	348.3	—
1946	—	334.9	—
1951	507.4	324.8	182.6
1961	473.7	286.6	187.1
1966	—	289.1	—
1971	489.8	289.3	200.5
1981	590.0	358.6	231.4
1991	746.8	471.6	275.2

Figures include those who are unemployed.

* The 1926 Census of the Irish Free State included female relatives assisting in agriculture for the first time in the occupied category, a total of 71,738 women. The adjusted figures exclude these women in order to make the 1926 figures directly comparable with 1911.
Source: 1841-1911 Census of Population, as adjusted by BOURKE 1993. However, these figures present some problems—see section III. For 1926-81 the source is the Population Census Irish Free State, Irish Republic and Northern Ireland.

a shift from agriculture, domestic service and employment within the family economy, to wage and salaried positions in industry or in services. Such changes had considerable significance for the female identity: women who worked for wages outside the home probably had a greater sense of autonomy than women who worked in a family business or family farm where they did not receive individual payment. The recent rise in the participation

Number of women with designated occupations
1841-1981

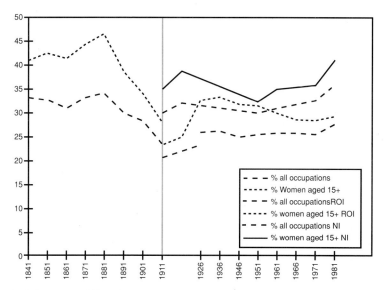

For ROI figures 1926 see Table 1

rate among married women may be even more significant. Since
World War II, and especially since the 'sixties, most developed
countries have seen a substantial rise in the proportion of
married women who work outside the home. They were attracted
into the labour market both by high wages and by a growing wish
to have more money available to spend on consumer goods or
leisure. In other countries this process has been closely associated
with a decline in the birth-rate (MINCER). In Northern Ireland
the proportion of married women working outside the home
began to rise in the 1960s; in the Irish Republic during the 1980s
the rise in the proportion of married women in the labour market
coincided with a sharp fall in fertility (WALSH 1993).

Any study of women's work in Ireland must pay particular
attention to Ulster. North-east Ulster ranks with areas such as
Lancashire in having had a high proportion of women in factory
employment during the nineteenth century. From 1841 the Ulster

counties which had strong textile or clothing sectors recorded the highest participation rates for women, and this pattern of a higher activity rate in Ulster relative to the rest of Ireland has persisted until the present day. Outside Ulster the proportion of women in the labour market appears to have been extremely low, by comparison with Britain. Many contemporary feminists have regarded access to paid employment and escape from domesticity as synonymous with women's liberation. Applying this point of view to nineteenth-century Ireland, several writers have concluded that falling employment in the second half of the nineteenth century signalled a deterioration in the condition of women (LEE 1979; FITZPATRICK 1987; NOLAN). However, we should beware of making judgements based on contemporary attitudes. Most women who engaged in paid employment in the past did so because of acute need; they had little if any choice in the type of work, or whether to work. The apparent fall in the number of women in the labour market in the late nineteenth century may reflect the fact that rising living standards allowed women to choose not to work as farm labourers or domestic servants (BOURKE 1993), or it may be due to changing practices by census enumerators which meant that some categories of women were no longer counted as 'occupied'. It may even indicate that the Irish economy was providing fewer jobs for women workers. While the proportion of Irish women in the paid labour-force in the Irish Republic may appear low by comparison with Britain or with Northern Ireland, this is partly a reflection of the importance of agriculture and the family economy where women's contribution has often been unrecognised. WALSH (1970) has pointed out that if farmers' wives had been counted as part of the female work-force the participation rate of Irish women in the 1960s would not have been significantly lower than in Britain.

II

WOMEN'S EMPLOYMENT IN PRE-FAMINE IRELAND

(a) *Domestic Industry*

Textiles provided the most important source of cash income for Irishwomen in the eighteenth and early nineteenth centuries. Spinning has traditionally been regarded as women's work and for many centuries Irish women spun wool and linen which was woven into cloth for family use. Yarn was sold in local markets and woollen yarn was being exported to Britain by the first half of the eighteenth century. Wool spinning was concentrated in the southern part of Ireland, in Cos. Cork, Kilkenny and Tipperary. Although the 1841 Census recorded that over 70,000 women were engaged in spinning wool and many of the 300,000 unspecified spinners may also have done so, the woollen industry was dwarfed by the rapid expansion of the linen industry during the eighteenth century. The various tasks within the linen industry were gender-specific: weaving was regarded as men's work because looms were heavy, though women wove a narrow cloth called bandle linen. Spinning was carried out by women and perhaps children, and as the industry needed at least four spinners to supply a weaver with yarn,[7] it was much more widespread than weaving. By the end of the eighteenth century linen spinning had spread from north-east Ulster through the remainder of the province into north Connacht and north Leinster. Most children were taught how to spin by their mothers; spinning wheels were not expensive and many were supplied free by the Linen Board. Wives and daughters of weavers supplied them with yarn and some weavers hired young live-in female servants to spin and to help with housework and farm chores. In the 1770s Arthur Young claimed that these servants earned 30/- (£1.50) for a half-year in addition to board and lodgings (CRAWFORD 1972, 1991). Jobbers bought yarn at markets in Sligo, Longford and other areas peripheral to the linen heartland and sold it to weavers in Armagh or Down.

Women's earnings from spinning varied widely because of variations in price, the number of hours which they worked and the quality of the yarn; finer counts obtained much higher prices than coarse yarn. One hank of yarn per day, less in the case of fine yarns, was regarded as the average. In the 1770s Arthur Young estimated that women in Sligo and Mayo earned from 4d. to 7d (1.5p to 3p approx.)per hank—figures which were not dramatically lower than the average daily earnings of male agricultural labourers at 6.5p.[8] Earnings from spinning appear to have peaked in the 1780s when yarn exports were at their highest level. The number of spinners continued to increase and this prevented earnings from rising: by the early 1800s earnings appear to have been similar to those for the 1770s; as prices had risen sharply, this amounted to a fall in real earnings.

Women spinners made an important contribution to family income, particularly on smaller farms and in households which lacked a cash income from weaving. In many parts of Connacht and north Leinster a woman's income from spinning was more regular than a man's earnings from agricultural labour, and women often provided the main cash income for a household. An account of Donegal in 1739 maintained that 'The Farmer generally contents himself with no more Land than is necessary to feed his Family; which he diligently tills; and Depends on the Industry of his Wife and Daughters to pay by their Spinning the Rent and Say (save?) up Riches'.[9]

Exports of linen yarn fell rapidly in the 1790s and businessmen began to import machine-spun cotton yarn from England which was woven into cloth. By the early nineteenth century it became possible to spin linen by machine, with one mill worker producing as much yarn as ten domestic spinners; the domestic industry was saved from extinction by the low cost of hand-spun yarn and the fact that fine linen could not be produced by machinery. The introduction of wet spinning in 1825, making it possible to spin fine linen by machine, meant that hand spinning was irretrievably doomed. English machine-spun yarn could now be bought for less than one-third of the price of hand-spun yarn. By the second decade of the nineteenth century women in outlying linen areas were finding it difficult to sell yarn. In 1816 few buyers attended Mullingar fair and prices dropped sharply. The major collapse appears to have taken place during the late 1820s. By the mid-1830s domestic spinning was said to have disappeared in Ballymoney, Co. Antrim; in Drumara, Co. Down, it was claimed that weekly earnings had fallen by two-thirds from the year 1815, from 4/6 to 5/- (22.5p to 25p) to 1/6 (7.5p) (POOR INQUIRY). The fact that some women continued to spin yarn despite derisory earnings indicates their acute need for money and the lack of alternative sources of income.

The collapse of domestic spinning was not unforeseen, given the precedent of cotton. In the early years of the nineteenth century the Linen Board offered bounties to encourage women to switch to weaving. There was plenty of work for weavers and the introduction of the flying-shuttle—first used for weaving cotton—made the job lighter and more suitable for women. This option, however, was only open to women living in areas where mill-spun yarn was readily available, such as east Ulster. Weavers' earnings also fell as more workers took up this trade. By the 1820s many Ulster weavers were emigrating with their families to Scottish towns such as Dundee, where the men worked as domestic weavers and women and children entered spinning mills. Single Irish women also sought work in Scottish textile mills(COLLINS 1981). New opportunities in domestic embroidery or flowering and in the linen mills only partly compensated for the decline in spinning and many families in west Ulster and Connacht became wholly dependent on agriculture.

(b) *Women in Pre-Famine Agriculture*
        Irish agriculture was transformed during the eighteenth century. The population rose from under 2m. in the 1740s to over 5m. by the end of the century. Food supplies expanded substantially to feed the rising population and wasteland was cleared and cultivated. The acreage devoted to potatoes, a labour-intensive crop, increased substantially and exports of butter, salt meats and grains rose. Dairying had traditionally been the major agricultural task carried out by women. They milked cows and made butter and in the early modern period when booleying or transhumance was common, women and children moved to upland pastures

during the summer months along with the cows and pigs while men tilled the fields on the lower ground.[10] Although the eighteenth century saw a rapid expansion of butter exports, particularly from Munster, the impact on women's employment remains obscure. DICKSON (1993) notes that 'herding sometimes, and milking invariably, were done by women, and in the great majority of cases labour was not drawn from outside the family for these tasks. It is indeed ironic that the hirers of cows were almost always men and presumably married men, whereas the main burden of dairying both in the field and at home fell on women'.[11] The income from selling butter probably accrued to the family, not to the individual worker, and we know little about women's role in the butter trade. Although there are frequent references to women who were engaged in retailing butter, sales on the Cork wholesale market appear to have been handled by men. Most dairy farms relied on family labour, though outsiders were hired when extra help was needed, particularly when children were young; and larger dairy farms depended on farm servants. In the early 1800s each of the five branches of the Ellward family in the Welsh (or Walsh) mountains in Co. Kilkenny employed ten servant boys and ten servant girls to tend 120 cows on each farm. Another Kilkenny dairy farm with twenty milch cows hired three dairy maids. Churning milk to make butter was regarded as women's work,[12] despite the fact that it was a physical-ly-demanding task. An early twentieth-century account declared that 'churning was a most inhuman labour to put women to, especially in the winter and when the whole milk was churned'; it also described 'women, often about to become mothers, labouring for a couple of hours, and almost fainting over their work'.[13] However as SNELL shows in the case of England, dairying was the only type of agricultural work to provide year-round paid employment for women; tillage only provided temporary work at peak times in the farming cycle.

The expansion of tillage in pre-Famine Ireland required substantial labour inputs. WAKEFIELD claimed that 'if four men, with two women following to bind, reap an acre (of wheat), it is called a good day's work'; according to another estimate eight men and four women could reap an acre of oats in one day. One farm in Tipperary engaged 42 men to dig an acre of potato ground; 12 girls and 8 boys to plant it; 12 men to shovel it, 12 women to weed it and 38 men to dig the potatoes for harvesting.[14] Women generally carried out the less skilled, subordinate, though back-breaking tasks which were often shared with boys. They cleared stones from fields prior to planting—one Co. Down farmer cited by BELL & WATSON estimated that it would take one woman four days to clear an acre; they weeded crops; planted potatoes on lazy beds or drills which had been dug by the men, carrying the seed in their aprons. Men dug out the mature potatoes which women harvested on their hands and knees. When hay was cut women made small lap cocks, 'each of which is equal to the quantity that a woman can twist round her arms in the shape of a muff'.[15] Flax was the most labour-intensive crop. When the land was ploughed women picked up the remaining clods of earth and either broke them up or dumped them at the edge of the field; they weeded the crop by hand, crawling over the ground on their knees—YOUNG claimed that ten women could weed an acre of flax in a day—and worked alongside men, pulling the mature crop and rippling it to save the seed. Flax was then steeped in dams—this was regarded as too heavy a task for women—but when the flax was removed women prepared it for drying and scutched it, beating the tough casing with a wooden 'beetle' to break it up. They then hung the flax on a block of wood and removed the broken casing by striking it with long wooden blades (CRAWFORD 1991).

Many of these tasks were carried out within the family economy. Evidence collected by the POOR INQUIRY suggests that by the 1830s there was very little paid agricultural employment open to women: 2-3 weeks work at harvest time and another 2-3 weeks setting and digging potatoes, and this was mainly carried out by younger single women who were 'disencumbered of children'. The amount of work available for women may have contracted in the early nineteenth century. Population growth meant more male labourers; there appears to have been a rise in the number of migrant labourers or spailpíní; falling agricultural prices after 1815 caused farmers to rely more heavily on family labour, while the increased use of ploughs instead of spades reduced the number of labourers needed. By the mid-1830s evidence collected by the POOR INQUIRY suggests that the only women with year-long employment were live-in servants. In many parts of the west of Ireland no paid agricultural employment was available to women. In Mohill, Co. Leitrim women were never hired for field work, though they assisted on family holdings. In Murrisk, Co. Mayo women were 'hardly ever employed for hire . . . where labourers are to be had for 6d (2.5p) and less no one wants women'. Even in Balrothery, Co. Dublin little paid employment was available; the respondent believed that most women were unable to carry out much outdoor work because they were suckling children. Paid work was available, if at all, for a maximum of 1-2 months in tillage areas of Co. Kilkenny, or for as little as ten days in Co. Mayo.[16] The 1841 Population Census asked each family to record the number of labourers employed and the duration of their employment. Surviving returns from Killashandra, Co. Cavan show that only six women were employed for an average of 29 days, four of them for less than a week (O'NEILL). Data collected by the POOR INQUIRY suggest that in the 1830s women earned from 50 to 66 per cent of male wage rates, or from 3 to 6d (1.25p to 2.5p) per day, excluding harvest work, when earnings were doubled. The budgets collected by the POOR INQUIRY suggest that women and children earned a maximum of 10/-(50p) in a year from agricultural work; earnings were much lower in western areas (CULLEN 1989).

Most women working in agriculture worked on family holdings. In cottier families O'NEILL has pointed out that 'women and children had little opportunity for employment on farms except during harvest, and even the head of the family was often not fully employed. The cot (i.e. plot of conacre land) gave the family a means of turning surplus labour directly into food without the need for cash to rent land'.[17] Women's work released men to take paid employment either locally or as migrant workers in England, a process which continued in western counties well into the present century. Income from poultry provided a partial compensation for lost earnings from spinning.[18] Most women kept from four to ten hens, earning an average of 10/-(50p) per annum from the sale of eggs and chickens. Eggs were often exchanged for soap, tea or tobacco. Average profit on a pig appears to have been 30/- (£1.50p). Cottiers who had only one or two acres could not feed a pig or even a small number of hens, and rearing poultry was not profitable if the family had to buy corn. Many labourers' wives were forbidden to keep hens because the fowl trespassed on the farmer's fields and ate his grain.

The total contribution made to family income by the combined earnings of women and children from farm labour, pigs and poultry, and domestic spinning varied widely depending on the opportunities available. In the poorest households where men had only irregular employment it could amount to over one-third of cash income (POOR INQUIRY), but it was less significant where men were in full-time employment. Women's earnings, however, were insufficient to sustain a family single-handed and the fate of widows was grim. Most labourers' widows lost the cabins they were occupying on their husband's death and became dependent on casual earnings from spinning, knitting or seasonal farm work. They were often driven to begging or prostitution.

(c) *Women's Work in Towns and Cities*

Although most women in urban areas depended on the family economy, towns and cities were believed to offer wider employment opportunities. CLARKSON (1978) has shown that in Armagh City in 1770 only 66 women (in a total population of almost 2,000) had independent occupations: they were engaged in domestic service, dealing, clothing manufacture, nursing and teaching. With the exception of textile towns such as Drogheda, Bandon, and Carrick-on-Suir, most manufacturing was concentrated in the countryside. CLARKSON (1993) estimates that approximately 1,200 women and girls may have been employed in woollen manufacture in Carrick-on-Suir in 1799. In most towns, however, the pattern of employment resembled Armagh. Women's work in late-eighteenth-century Dublin was concentrated in domestic and personal service, including food and drink, together with textiles, clothing and dealing. An illustrated broadsheet dating from the 1770s and titled *The Dublin Cries* depicts the Curds and Whey Woman; the Woman selling Hot Cakes; the Rag Woman; the Girl Selling Vegetables; the Girl Selling Cherries; and the Fish Woman.[19] BROPHY suggests that women had access to a wider range of occupations in an era dominated by the family economy than in later times. Women controlled some businesses in eighteenth-century Dublin as in other towns. Many were widows of previous proprietors, though in the case of some textile or clothing businesses there was no apparent record of previous male ownership. CLARKSON'S study of Armagh suggests that such women were exceptional, and the argument that women in later generations faced a narrower range of job opportunities remains unproven; such analysis also fails to recognise that family businesses continued to be important in the Irish economy until recent years. Women were generally excluded from formal apprenticeships and from skilled trades, though some acquired the necessary skills within the family economy and the skill of milliner appears to have been monopolised by women. As the population grew, competition for jobs increased and BROPHY shows that from the mid-eighteenth century journeymen combinations demanded that women be excluded from trades such as worsted weaving and tailoring. Most women living in towns filled less skilled, poorly paid occupations. In the mid-1830s women in the Cork City parish of Shandon sorted feathers, prepared offal for market, and collected wash and grain from the city distillery to feed their pigs. Others sold old clothes, shoes, potatoes, vegetables, and dairy products. Straw bonnet-making, dress-making, stay-making, glove-making and the preparation of feathers and down were the main occupations in the nearby parish of St. Peter and Paul where, according to evidence given to the POOR INQUIRY, *comparatively few* women earned a comfortable subsistence and the majority were described as having 'a scanty and precarious one'.[20]

The 1821 Census only tabulated occupations of male household heads, so the 1841 Census provides the first statistical data on women's employment. The Census records the work carried out by cash-earning women, but almost certainly omits from the occupied labour force farmers' or cottiers' wives who occasionally sold eggs or poultry and those engaged in intermittent agricultural labour. The data suggest that 60 per cent of women with specified occupations were engaged in textiles and clothing; 22 per cent as domestic servants; and 13 per cent in food and agriculture. Of the half a million women engaged in spinning, more than 100,000 lived in the province of Connacht, though many of these spinners were earning little income by this stage. The highest rates of recorded female employment were found in areas with substantial employment in domestic textiles: all Ulster counties reported above-average participation rates, as did Leitrim and Westmeath; the lowest participation rates were recorded in counties with little textile employment (SEE MAP 1).

The contribution which women made to household income was most important in labouring families, where questions of female status or equality were overshadowed by a struggle for survival. Although female spinners appear to have had some discretionary spending power and earnings from poultry were often spent on luxuries such as tea, soap or tobacco, the heavy labour and begging done by many labouring women is unlikely to have enhanced their status. WAKEFIELD complained that 'Women in Ireland are treated more like beasts of burden than rational beings, and although I never saw one yoked to a plough . . . I have seen them degraded in a manner disgraceful to the other sex, and shocking to humanity. In the country they are subjected to all the drudgery generally performed by men; setting potatoes, digging turf, and the performance of the most laborious occupations. I have often watched them with the utmost attention, but never heard a woman disobey the command of her husband, or repine at his orders'.[21]

Plentiful employment for women and children in domestic industry has been associated with earlier marriages and accelerated population growth in other parts of Europe (FISCHER). Although MOKYR, using the 1841 Census, does not find a conclusive link between cottage industry and the propensity of women to marry, areas with a strong linen industry experienced above-average population growth in late-eighteenth-century Ireland; from the 1820s, however, deteriorating prospects triggered a sharp rise in emigration from textile areas such as Ulster and north Connacht.

III

THE POST-FAMINE ECONOMY

The population of Ireland fell by over 1.5m. between 1841 and 1851 as a result of Famine-related deaths, emigration and lower fertility. The proportion of women in the labour force fell as a result of the collapse of domestic spinning. The number of female spinners fell from over half a million in 1841 to 112,000 ten years later. According to the Population Census the proportion of women in the labour force increased during the years 1851-81, only to fall sharply over the next thirty years. BOURKE (1993) attributes this fall to a boom in the rural economy, which enabled women to opt out of paid employment in favour of unpaid domestic duties within the family. However, the scale of the loss—more than one female job in five in the years 1881-91— is puzzling and contrasts sharply with the trend over the previous two decades. It seems possible that the decline was largely the result of different practices by Census enumerators. The fall in the number of occupied women occurred almost entirely among women aged over 24: one-quarter of women aged 45 and over 'lost' their jobs, as did a slightly smaller proportion of those aged 25-44. Four-fifths of all job 'losses' occurred in the vague category 'others engaged in service' where employment fell from 139,092 in 1881 to 1,317 in 1891; the balance can be explained by declining numbers of domestic servants and female agricultural labourers. 'Others engaged in service' was an undefined category which included female family members, such as sisters and aunts who helped with household chores. These women did not 'opt' out of paid employment; most would only have received board and keep within a household. The only change occurring between 1881 and 1891 was in how they were classified by Census enumerators.

What then happened to women's employment in post-Famine Ireland? Total employment fell for both men and women. Women's paid employment in agriculture fell, though this had only accounted for one job in eight in 1841. The most significant

18

loss in female employment resulted from the collapse of domestic spinning, which was underway before the Famine. In some parts of Ulster the impact was cushioned by the growth of factory employment and by new forms of domestic industry. Elsewhere there were few alternative occupations and the loss of women's earnings from domestic industry coupled with declining employment for male agricultural labourers ended the prospect of early marriage for many landless or near-landless couples and pointed both men and women towards emigration: approximately one-third of young men and women emigrated in the immediate post-Famine decades, with the highest concentrations coming from areas with below-average female employment. Changes in women's employment in the post-Famine decades were probably more gradual than BOURKE suggests and the regional employment patterns evident in 1861 are similar to those in 1911. By 1861 the highest proportions of working women were in Cos. Antrim, Armagh and Down and urban areas such as Dublin City and suburbs; the lowest were in the five Connacht counties and in parts of Leinster (SEE p. 21). Beyond the industrialised areas of Ulster and the cities of Dublin and Cork, women's work outside the family economy was largely limited to domestic service.

(a) *Agriculture*

In 1841 only 12.5 per cent of occupied women were engaged in the agricultural or food sectors. By 1911 13.7 per cent of occupied women were engaged in agriculture; women's recorded employment in agriculture fell at a lesser rate than total female employment. Post-Famine agriculture increasingly relied on family members rather than hired labourers. However, Census peculiarities, such as excluding farmers' wives and other female relatives from the agricultural workforce while male relatives living on farms were counted, means that the figures are seriously distorted. According to the Census there were only 4,000 female agricultural labourers in 1911. The number of female farmers rose steadily until 1901, when, according to the Census, they accounted for over three-quarters of all women in agriculture and one in five of all Leinster farmers. Most were middle-aged or elderly widows or single women, who appear to have been

Females aged 15+ with stated occupations as Precentage of Female Population aged 15+
1841

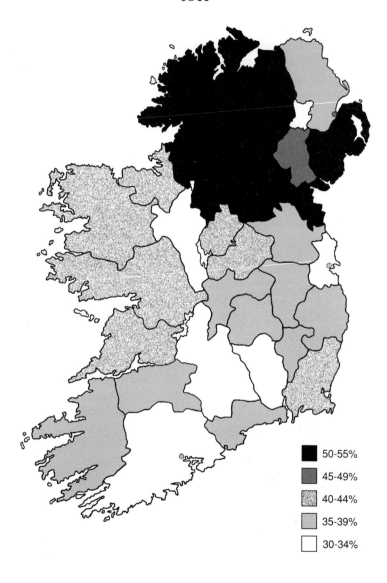

50-55%

45-49%

40-44%

35-39%

30-34%

Females aged 15+ with stated occupations as Precentage of Female Population aged 15+ 1861

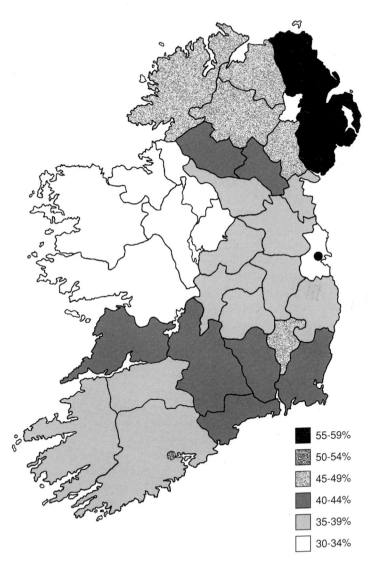

55-59%

50-54%

45-49%

40-44%

35-39%

30-34%

reluctant to hand over the family farm to a son; over 80 per cent of Leinster women farmers were aged over 45. Women farmers were less common in western counties where the transmission of farms between the generations appears to have been accomplished more smoothly (FITZPATRICK 1980). The proportion fell in 1911, perhaps because elderly women relinquished control to qualify for an old-age pension (GUINNANE 1993).

Women farmers and farm labourers were only a small part of the *actual* female agricultural labour force. Fortunately the 1871 Census provides a once-off record of the involvement of farm wives and female family labour in agriculture. In 1871 over 30 per cent of agricultural workers were women, almost two-thirds of them farmers' wives, who far outstripped other female relatives (18.5 per cent) and women labourers and farm servants (16 per cent). More than two-thirds of assisting daughters were under 25 years of age, and only one in ten was aged over 35 years. The overwhelming majority of paid female workers were farm servants: young single workers who were recruited for six-month periods at hiring fairs and who lived in the farm-house. Most were daughters of farm labourers or small farmers, whose earnings were an important source of supplementary income; many subsequently emigrated (BREEN). The Agricultural Census taken in June 1912, which included part-time workers and female relatives, showed that women accounted for just under one-quarter of the labour-force on all farms, irrespective of size. Eighty-six per cent of women engaged in agriculture were farmers or family members, with the balance almost evenly divided between permanent and temporary labourers; most hired labour was found on larger farms.[22]

The range of farm tasks carried out by women appears to have narrowed after the Famine as a result of the decline in tillage and increased mechanisation, though women continued to help in the fields during peak times such as hay-making, harvest time, potato planting and picking, as numerous surviving photographs indicate (BELL & WATSON; HILL & POLLOCK). Most surviving descriptions of women working outdoors originate in the areas along the western seaboard which came under the jurisdiction of the Congested Districts Board. In Ballycroy, Co. Mayo in 1896,

'The women besides all the ordinary domestic duties, carding, spinning etc., take part in field labour with the men, and gather sea-weed for manure; the only kind of work they do not engage in is cutting turf'.[23] In other western communities women harvested turf and gathered seaweed for kelp making, which involved wading into the sea below the low tide mark. The range of heavy agricultural tasks carried out by women in western counties (within the family economy) should be seen as a continuation of pre-Famine practices when they took charge of the family plot while men sought paid employment. Migratory labour in Scotland and England meant that adult men were absent for up to six months in the year from many parts of Mayo and Donegal; younger males were hired out to larger farmers, while men, and occasionally women, also took jobs on relief schemes or road works. The persistence of the intensive farming practices of pre-Famine Ireland, plus the lack of machinery and beasts of burden—there are numerous descriptions of women carrying heavy loads on their backs—would have increased women's outdoor work.

Elsewhere women appear to have been largely confined to the farm-yard, except during peak times in the farming year. They combined housework with farm duties, milking cows, feeding pigs and calves and caring for poultry, which remained an important source of supplementary earnings until the 1950s. Egg-money was often a woman's only source of discretionary income and BOURKE (1993) shows that women were loath to sell eggs to creameries because payment would be combined with the farm's income from milk which was not under the woman's control.

Creameries brought about the most dramatic change in women's farm employment. Milking cows and churning butter were long-established women's tasks and the large dairy farm of the O'Brien family described in *The Farm by Lough Gur* (CARBERY) employed numerous dairy maids. Butter-making, which was supervised by Mrs. O'Brien and her daughter, was on a scale comparable to a medium-sized industry. The invention of the centrifugal separator transferred butter-making from the home to the creamery, where most jobs were filled by men. This appears to have resulted in a substantial loss of female agricultural employment in the 1880s and 1890s. Although cows still had to be milked, BOURKE (1993) shows that the end of domestic butter-making left insufficient full-time employment for dairy maids; if the family could not milk the cows, farmers increasingly hired male labourers who would combine milking with general farm tasks. Although dairy farms continued to provide more work for women than other types of agriculture, the work was usually undertaken by female relatives; the 1912 Agricultural Census shows that dairy counties recorded the highest proportion of women relative to men in agriculture.

The value of agricultural output rose in the late nineteenth century at a time when the numbers dependent on farming were in decline. Wives, daughters and unmarried sisters appear to have given greater attention to housekeeping and cookery. Baking soda bread became part of the daily ritual; houses grew larger, parlours, complete with pictures, ornaments and good furniture, became common. In adopting such practices, Irish rural women were following the pattern of middle-class women both in Ireland and elsewhere. Daughters of middling and larger farmers often remained at home helping with these duties and awaiting marriage; if no husband materialised they continued as unpaid housekeepers. On smaller holdings poverty dictated that all should contribute to family income, hence the tendency for young girls from small western farms to be hired as farm servants, or to emigrate as seasonal workers. Although families appear to have been reluctant to see daughters travel to Scotland or England as seasonal workers, gangs of girls left Achill and Donegal in the late nineteenth century (O'DOWD). Others emigrated and sent home remittances: SYNGE claimed that in the poorest districts of Connemara 'many families are only kept from pauperism by the money that is sent home to them by daughters or sisters who are now servant-girls in New York'.[24]

(b) *Women and Manufacturing Industry*
(i) *Domestic Industry*

Young single women could augment family income by permanent or temporary migration, an option not open to married women, widows or older single women living in the countryside. Many writers in the nineteenth century believed that domestic industry offered women the best of both worlds: an opportunity to earn money while simultaneously coping with child-care and domestic duties. However, the collapse of domestic spinning in the first half of the nineteenth century narrowed women's options; by 1861 there were only 13,000 female spinners in Connacht, a drop of over 100,000 on 1841, and domestic spinning had virtually disappeared in Ulster. COLLINS (1988) shows that by 1841 alternative industries such as lace-making, crochet, embroidery and flowering had been started in many areas with mixed success. The sewn muslin trade and muslin embroidery developed in Ulster in the 1820s as an offshoot of cotton spinning using machine-made thread and had spread into west Ulster by the 1830s. Warehouses trained workers, distributed materials and collected finished goods. By 1851 almost 100,000 Ulster women were engaged either in embroidery or sewed muslin work. However, the industry declined from the late 1850s as a result of changing fashion and the crisis in the cotton industry during the American civil war. A growing market subsequently emerged for hand-embroidered linen sheets, table-cloths and handkerchiefs, though employment never equalled the levels attained in 1851.

The Ulster flowering and embroidery industries were established on a commercial basis and produced items for which there was a wide demand. Many lace and crochet industries were founded by philanthropists on a less secure basis. Patrons tended to be the wives and sisters of clergymen and landlords or members of religious communities. Carrickmacross lace was inaugurated c. 1820 by a clergyman's wife, developed by a landlord's sister and eventually came under the care of the Sisters of St. Louis. There was a virtual epidemic of similar enterprises during the 1840s and many of them exhibited work at the 1851 International Exhibition. Religious orders such as the sisters of Mercy and the Poor Clares taught lace and embroidery in the industrial schools under their control (ELIZABETH BOYLE). From the 1890s the Congested Districts Board, the Department of Agriculture, the co-operative movement and Lady Aberdeen's Irish Industries Association were all engaged in promoting lace-making, crochet work, knitting and similar industries.[25] Yet the economic value of these enterprises remains questionable. The fortunes of Limerick lace were not untypical; it claimed to employ 1,900 at its peak around 1840, but a brief period of success was followed by long decline. Patrons exaggerated the earning potential of workers. Sales were often excessively dependent on the goodwill of patrons' friends; agents involved in more commercial operations were alleged to exploit workers. Many were local shopkeepers who forced workers to spend their earnings from knitting or crochet work on over-priced tea from their store. When a particular type of hand-work became fashionable, the skill spread widely, and the market became saturated with the result that earnings fell. Irish workers had to compete with domestic lace and embroidery industries in Belgium, Switzerland and Austria. Earnings appear to have been low, though as piece-work was the norm it is difficult to be precise. BOURKE concludes that 'generally, average wages between 1908 and 1910 ranged between 4/- (20p) and 7/- (35p) in home industries as diverse as Donegal embroidery, lace making in congested districts and Limerick lace'.[26] A report on domestic industry in Ulster in the early twentieth century carried out on behalf of the anti-sweating campaign by IRWIN stated that in many cases wages did not exceed 1d per hour, with steady work only yielding 'about 7/- (35p) per week'. The author described one woman who embroidered 'elaborate sprays' on each corner of a handkerchief at the rate of 1/6 (7.5p) per dozen; it took her 'almost a day' to complete two. These earnings compared unfavourably with the estimated weekly earnings of domestic spinners in the late eighteenth century. Many women used their earnings from domestic industry to emigrate. Women found it difficult to combine domestic industry with family duties and BOURKE (1993) shows that the majority of domestic workers in Co. Fermanagh were single women, heads of household or sisters, aunts, nieces or mothers attached to other family units. Despite the low level of earnings, income from domestic industry often proved vital to the survival of both rural and urban households. The Baseline reports carried out by the Congested Districts Board in the early 1890s recorded the importance of knitting, lace-making, embroidery, sewing collars and tweed in supplementing household incomes throughout Co. Donegal. Women in Inishowen earned an estimated £13 per annum from sewing collars, almost double the £7 which women in the Rosses earned from knitting (MURPHY).

The most successful domestic industry of post-Famine Ireland was the mass production of shirts, collars and women's underclothes. Unlike lace making it was not based on the revival of 'traditional' skills but employed modern mass-production techniques to provide the growing number of clerical workers with white shirts and a supply of detachable collars and cuffs which could be changed every day. Shirt making developed in Derry city in the 1850s and expanded to employ thousands of outworkers in the county and in adjoining parts of Donegal. The shirts were cut out to standard sizes in factories within the city. The pieces were assembled by women, who worked at home often in the company of other women (NEILL). Firms opened agencies or outstations in adjoining towns and villages, where work was handed out, completed work was collected and workers collected their pay. In 1856 the Scottish firm Tillie and Henderson introduced the first sewing machines to the area. One woman using a hand-powered machine was estimated to equal the output of six hand sewers; out-workers bought machines from manufacturers on easy payments. Early machines could only tackle plain seaming and collars and cuffs continued to be sewn by hand. In 1867 approximately 2,000 workers were employed in factories cutting-out, laundering and packing shirts, and a further 10,000 outworkers were employed throughout Cos. Derry and Donegal. By 1902 the industry employed approximately 18,000 factory employees and 80,000 outworkers, 80 per cent of them women. With the development of steam-powered sewing machines, production gradually shifted to the factories, though this trend was masked by the industry's continued expansion (COLLINS 1988; OLLEREN-SHAW). The Belfast area also had an important making-up industry, while in Dublin smaller numbers of women and men working at home supplied city department stores with shirts and suits. Other women made clothes for private clients. The 1891 Census recorded 13,691 female dressmakers in Dublin city; fewer than 5,000 of these appear to have worked in factories or workshops (DALY 1984). Domestic workers probably outnumbered factory workers prior to World War One. Although outworkers engaged by shirt factories faced more stable market conditions than lacemakers, competition between firms, plus the elastic supply of seamstresses, kept wages low, and hours and working conditions were unregulated. An inquiry carried out in 1911 by the British Home Office into conditions of employment in the making-up trades informed the principal employers that some of the wages paid to less skilled outworkers 'were so small as to amount to underpayment' and recommended the establishment of a trade board to fix minimum rates of pay.[27]

(ii) *Women and Factory Employment*

The female factory worker is so often seen as synonymous with women's work that there is a danger of forgetting that factories and mills employed only a minority of working women, even in countries more industrialised than Ireland. The number of jobs created in factories was substantially less than the numbers lost in domestic industry, despite the fact that Ireland's industrial revolution was based on linen—an industry which was dominated by women.[28] Most linen mills and factories clustered in north-east Ulster to take advantage of external economies. For similar reasons shirt-making factories tended to locate in the north-west of the province. Most female factory workers outside Ulster were also employed in the clothing and textiles industries. According to the 1907 CENSUS OF PRODUCTION woollen mills employed 1,700 women; most plants were small and the greatest concentration was in the Cork area(CRONIN). The only other factory-based industries employing more than 1,000 women in 1907 were biscuits and baking and laundries. Jacob's biscuit factory in Dublin, with approximately 2,000 women workers, was the largest employer of women outside the clothing and textile industries.

The first modern factories in Ireland were cotton-spinning plants established in the late eighteenth century in Balbriggan, Prosperous, Stratford-on-Slaney and Belfast. Cotton mills continued to be established in Belfast until the 1830s. Women and children provided a source of cheap labour, and were regarded as more amenable to discipline than men and capable of carrying out repetitive manufacturing processes without serving a lengthy apprenticeship. Two-thirds of the workers in the Belfast cotton mills were women (GEARY). By the late 1820s the technical problems associated with machine-spinning flax had been surmounted and linen mills began to supplant cotton. By 1850 there were 33 mills in Belfast and hinterland, 5 in west Ulster and only 6 south of the province. They employed over 20,000 workers, the majority of them women or juveniles.[29] Weaving remained a domestic industry until the 1850s when it was mechanised to meet expanding demand. The major spurt in mechanisation took place during the 1860s when linen experienced a boom period because of difficulties with cotton supplies as a result of the American civil war. Handloom weaving was traditionally carried out by men; in the factories the process passed to women. By the 1870s over 70,000 workers were employed, which was close to the pre-1914 peak employment of 74,000 workers in 1910 (BOYLE, OLLERENSHAW).

As factory jobs emerged in Belfast and domestic employment disappeared in rural areas women moved into the city from adjoining counties. Many young women moved with their families; others left home to live in lodging-houses presided over by an older woman or boarded with relatives who helped them find work. Mill and factory employment meant a new degree of regulation and discipline. Work began at 6 a.m., and latecomers were either locked out or fined. Workers were subjected to detailed, often vexatious supervision, generally by male overseers, with fines imposed for trivial offences such as whistling. The working hours of women and young persons in textile plants were limited by law. A ten-hour day applied from 1847; in the early 'fifties it was specified that the normal working day should be between the hours of 6 a.m. and 6 p.m. with meal-breaks; from 1874 a 56-hour week applied, ten hours on weekdays with a half-day on Saturday.

BOYLE suggests that the wages of female linen workers increased at a slower rate than those of unskilled men. This may reflect the fact that there appears to have been no shortage of women workers. In 1901 Belfast contained 1,290 adult women per 1,000 men; in the 20-29 age group there were four women for every three men. Among migrants in the 15-24 age-group, women outnumbered men by almost three to two (HEPBURN & COLLINS).

Working conditions in the linen industry were unhealthy: spinning rooms were very hot and damp to prevent threads snapping, and this made them an ideal breeding ground for TB. Flax fibres covered spinners with a permanent layer of dust and caused serious lung disease. Fatigue and carelessness led to accidents (ARMSTRONG). Weaving factories were cleaner and, as NORA CONNOLLY O'BRIEN discovered, the workers regarded themselves as superior. They were paid by piece-rates (often regarded as the sign of a skilled worker), whereas spinners received a weekly wage. Women working in dress-making also saw themselves as superior to mill-workers, because their work was cleaner and presumably healthier. Despite the long hours and poor working conditions, oral evidence collected by MESSENGER, admittedly during the present century when conditions had improved, combines recollections of harsh conditions with stories of fun and friendship, a reminder of the important social dimension which working outside the home could provide. Indeed, there is substantial, if fragmentary, evidence that women often regarded paid work as offering important opportunities for sociability, whether in the factory or in the home. Out-workers in the shirt industry often gathered in one person's home so that they could gossip while they sewed, while GREY cites WAKEFIELD'S description of young women who travelled a considerable distance carrying a spinning wheel on their head in order to 'spin, sing and converse' together.

(c) *Domestic Service*

Many domestic servants seem to have regarded their isolated working conditions as a disadvantage. The proportion of Irishwomen who worked as domestic servants rose in the second half of the nineteenth century, though many of them worked in New York or Boston rather than in Cork, Dublin or Belfast (DINER, KATZMAN). Data in the Census suggest that the number of female servants rose until 1881 when they accounted for almost half of all women with stated occupations. Thereafter the number declined, though this may be largely due to changing practices by Census enumerators. Nevertheless domestic service accounted for one-third of all occupied women in 1911 and remained a significant source of employment in the Irish Free State until after World War II. From the mid-nineteenth century there was a growing demand for servants from the expanding urban middle class living in Dublin suburbs such as Rathmines (DALY 1984). Service offered most young women who left the Irish countryside both a home and the only reliable opportunity of earning a living. Few unskilled females earned sufficient money to pay for board and lodging. For this reason orphans and girls in reformatories or industrial schools were commonly given a domestic training before being placed with a family. Parents often preferred their daughters to go into service rather than into a factory because service was regarded as a form of protected employment: the young worker (often in her early 'teens) lived in a family and her private life was supervised. Housekeeping skills would come in useful when the young woman married, whereas factory girls were believed to be utterly deficient in that regard.

Most servants working in Dublin came from adjoining counties. HEARN shows that many senior staff in large country houses were English or Scottish. Training took place on the job and some women rose from positions as general servants to become parlour maids or cooks. Despite the images of life in the 'Big House' the typical servant worked in a one- or two-servant household. Middle-class families in the late nineteenth century generally kept two servants, but many servants were employed by families who could barely afford their wages but needed help with heavy cleaning or child-care. Living conditions varied considerably. FRANK O'CONNOR's mother experienced utter cruelty and near-starvation in some posts; in another household she was virtually a member of the family. Wages also varied from £3 to £10 per annum in the 1880s, depending on age and experience; the highest wages were paid in upper-class households which had a large staff. Taking the value of board and lodging into consideration, servants were among the highest-paid women workers at that time. Many succeeded in saving a high proportion of their earnings. Although almost half of domestic servants were aged less than 25 years, HEARN claims that they were less likely to marry than other women; whether this was because service gave them the option of remaining single, or because they found it difficult to meet prospective husbands, is a matter for speculation. Old age could prove a grim time: their work was their home, and many ended their days in the workhouse (DALY 1984). Losing a job meant losing a home.

Why did the number of servants apparently decline from 1881? Real wages rose more slowly at the end of the century than wages for alternative occupations, which may indicate that there was less demand for servants, though repeated middle-class complaints about a servant shortage belie this. The small size of the Irish middle class limited the market for servants. BOURKE (1991/1993), writing about rural Ireland, suggests that women increasingly opted for unpaid domestic service in the family home instead of paid service for strangers; as DINER shows, others preferred to seek better-paid positions in the United States or in Britain. For girls from the west of Ireland, Boston was often less foreign than Dublin.

(d) *Women's Employment in Urban Ireland: Some Comparisons*
    Before World War I the overwhelming majority of women with recorded occupations were poor; the only exceptions were a small number of female professionals and commercial clerks. Women in middle-class families, and some in skilled working-class families, did not work outside the home, irrespective of marital status. A sample taken from the 1901 Belfast Census enumeration forms reveals that 56 per cent of Catholic females aged 12 and over had a stated occupation, compared with 43 per cent of women from the more prosperous Presbyterian community (HEPBURN & COLLINS). Child workers invariably came from impoverished families: MESSENGER relates a family's distress when a birth certificate revealed that a child was not old enough to start work in a linen mill. For families which depended on female or child earnings, Ulster cities offered better opportunities than Dublin or Cork where most women were employed in domestic service and

dealing. Younger women were much more likely to be employed in Belfast or Derry, in part because both cities had a higher proportion of working-class families, but also because jobs were available in textile and clothing plants.

For most women living in towns and cities employment outside the home was not a life-long experience. Most women who worked in linen plants were young: in 1871 10 per cent were aged under 15 and 50 per cent were aged between 15 and 25; the proportions were almost identical in 1911. COHEN shows that in 1901 two-thirds of the adult female workers in the textile plant in Gilford, Co. Down were aged between 18 and 30. The overwhelming majority of women factory workers in Cork were under 25 years of age (CRONIN).

Women textile workers appear to have been unique in continuing to work in a factory or mill after marriage. In 1871 over one-quarter of women employed in linen and cotton manufacture were married. Conditions for such women were extremely difficult: many worked until the eve of child-birth and returned to work after a short absence—a practice which ruled out breast-feeding and left their infants vulnerable to serious illness. These women continued in paid employment because the family income was inadequate. Skilled male workers could afford to keep their wives at home and their children at school; the combined wages of a labourer and a female textile worker barely equalled that of a skilled shipyard worker. According to COLLINS (1982), in Belfast in 1901 one Protestant wife in ten and one Catholic wife in five were listed as having a specific occupation. In the parish of Tullylish, Co. Down, the location of the Gilford/Dunbarton textile plant, one woman in five with a resident husband worked in a factory and over 40 per cent of widows were in employment (COHEN). Although many married women left work following the birth of a first child, more than one Belfast Catholic wife in five and one Protestant wife in ten with young children continued in paid employment, because demands on family income were at their maximum at this stage. Where possible families preferred to send children to work and keep a wife at home. In Belfast the proportion of working wives declined when children were old enough to work and remained low as long as there were resident

Occupational Profile of Female Labour-Force 1911, %

BELFAST

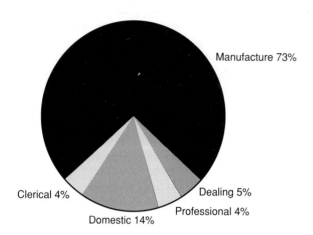

CORK

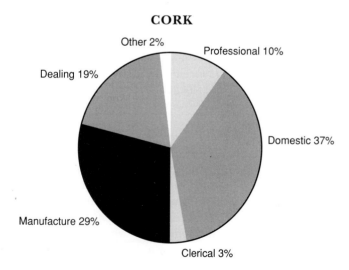

Occupational Profile of Female Labour-Force 1911, %

DERRY

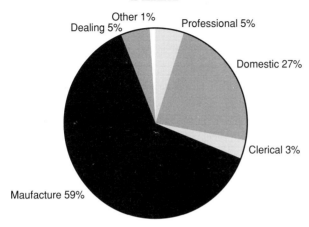

Other 1%
Dealing 5%
Professional 5%
Domestic 27%
Clerical 3%
Maufacture 59%

DUBLIN

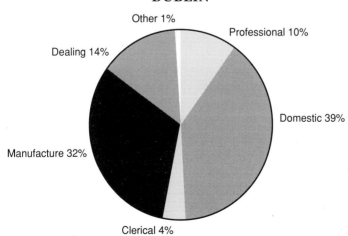

Other 1%
Professional 10%
Dealing 14%
Domestic 39%
Manufacture 32%
Clerical 4%

Female labour-Force Participation by Age, 1911%

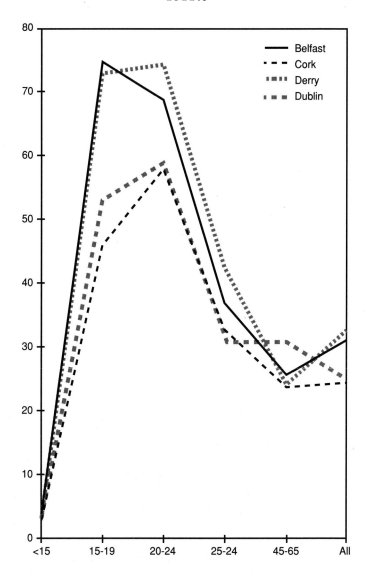

Occupational Profile of Female Labour Force
1911%

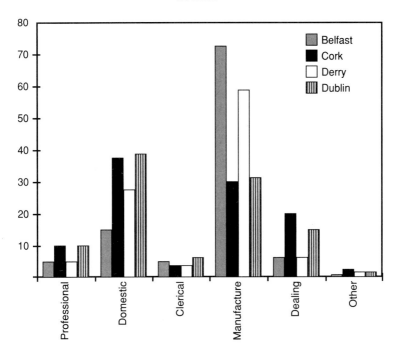

children to supplement family income, but many elderly women re-entered the labour market after their children left home. Other married women in Belfast chose jobs which appeared more compatible with family duties, such as sewing, charring or laundry work, though in the process they became part of a less secure secondary labour market. In Dublin and Cork wives and widows of labouring families had to rely on casual dealing, taking in laundry or cleaning houses; these employment patterns persisted after Independence (KEARNS). Dublin charities frequently supplied widows or wives of incapacitated men with sufficient money to enable them to deal in fish, fruit, vegetables or delft. However, few widows could earn sufficient money to support a family and many charities placed children in orphanages leaving

tional opportunities, all teachers and nurses suffered restrictions on their personal lives. Trainee nurses were required to live-in under regulations as draconian as those suffered by many domestic servants. Many nurses and teachers were required to resign on marriage. Secondary school teachers were poorly paid; in 1905 women teachers earned less than £1 per week, which was approximately the wage of an unskilled labourer. Both male and female teachers lacked security of employment. Qualified teachers were often displaced by cheaper, unqualified ex-pupils, both lay and religious (COOLAHAN). Although a system of registration was introduced in 1918, unregistered teachers continued to outnumber registered women teachers during the 1930s. Few women had entered the higher professions prior to World War One; although the Royal College of Physicians (Ireland) opened their examinations to women in 1877 and the first women graduated from the Irish College of Surgeons in 1890, there were only 33 qualified female medical doctors in Ireland in 1911, though the census recorded 68 female medical students. In 1911 there were no female lawyers, and a sole female architect or assistant (probably an assistant). In 1919 the Sex Disqualification Act gave women access to careers as solicitors or barristers.[31] BARKER describes the horror in the Institute of Chartered Accountants when the first woman applied for admission as a student in 1901. Restrictions on the admission of women were not lifted until 1920; the first woman member was admitted in 1925.

IV

WOMEN'S EMPLOYMENT, NORTH AND SOUTH, POST 1922.

In the 1920s the proportion of women in paid employment was much higher in Northern Ireland than in the Irish Free State, though counties such as Fermanagh had much more in common with the latter area than with north-east Ulster. The family economy loomed much larger in the Irish Free State than in Northern Ireland. According to the 1926 Census 40 per cent of women either worked on their own account or as assisting relatives and over 60 per cent were engaged in either agriculture or domestic service. According to the 1926 Irish Free State Census, more than one-third of women were engaged in agriculture, a much higher figure than in any previous census because all female relatives assisting on farms were included in the agricultural workforce with the exception of farmers' wives. If they had also been included the dominance of agriculture would have been considerably greater. In Northern Ireland, by comparison, less than one-quarter of women worked in either agriculture or domestic service. The proportion of women in employment was static or in decline throughout Ireland until the 1960s. Women in the Irish Free State probably fared better during the 1930s, whereas World War II brought limited benefits to women in Northern Ireland.

Between 1961 and 1981 the proportion of women in the labour market in the Irish Republic fell, whereas in Northern Ireland the female participation rate rose sharply. Most of the increase consisted of part-time workers who tended to be married; by the 1980s one third of women in paid employment in Northern Ireland worked part-time. By 1981 the proportion of women in the labour force in Northern Ireland was almost identical to the British figure and both areas had a significant proportion of women in part-time employment. By 1981 over 44.8 per cent of married women in Northern Ireland were in the labour market, more than double the percentage in the Irish Republic (20.4 per cent) (JEFFERSON, TREWSDALE).

41

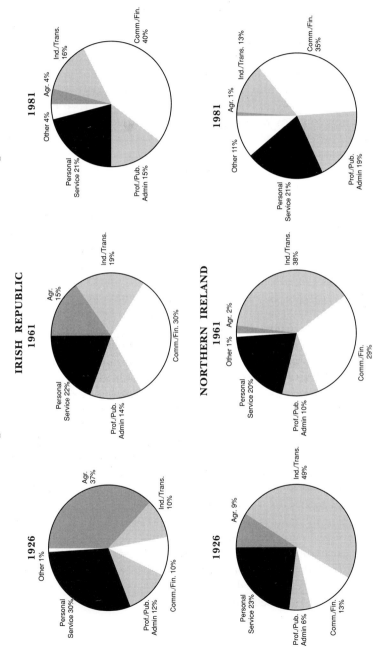

Female Occupations in Northern Ireland and Irish Republic

IRISH REPUBLIC

1981

Comm./Fin. 40%
Ind./Trans. 16%
Agr. 4%
Other 4%
Personal Service 21%
Prof./Pub. Admin 15%

1961

Ind./Trans. 19%
Agr. 15%
Comm./Fin. 30%
Personal Service 22%
Prof./Pub. Admin 14%

1926

Agr. 37%
Other 1%
Ind./Trans. 10%
Comm./Fin. 10%
Personal Service 30%
Prof./Pub. Admin 12%

NORTHERN IRELAND

1981

Comm./Fin. 35%
Ind./Trans. 13%
Agr. 1%
Other 11%
Personal Service 21%
Prof./Pub. Admin 19%

1961

Ind./Trans. 38%
Agr. 2%
Other 1%
Comm./Fin. 29%
Personal Service 20%
Prof./Pub. Admin 10%

1926

Ind./Trans. 49%
Agr. 9%
Comm./Fin. 13%
Personal Service 23%
Prof./Pub. Admin 6%

The contrast between the rising participation rate among women in Northern Ireland after 1961 and twenty years of decline in the Irish Republic is interesting, given that for much of this period the Irish Republic achieved a higher rate of economic growth. However, in the Irish Republic the economic boom of the early 'sixties led to a decline in the proportion of women who were in the labour market. Rising living standards resulted in early marriages, a higher marriage rate and a baby boom which caused women to withdraw from paid employment (WALSH) at a time when married women in Northern Ireland were taking part-time jobs. The contrast between both parts of Ireland may reflect the absence of a tradition of wage-earning married women in the Republic, or perhaps differing attitudes on the part of employers and workers to part-time work. Marital fertility, hence family size, remained much higher in the Irish Republic than in other parts of Europe, which would have made it more difficult for married women to re-enter the labour force. Women in the Irish Republic have one of the lowest documented levels of part-time employment in the European Union: in 1984 only one woman in nine who held a job worked part-time (BLACKWELL). However, in reality this figure may be too low: many part-time employees work outside the tax and social welfare system.

The stagnation or decline in women's employment in the Irish Republic from the 1920s until the 1980s masks significant changes in the status and age of working women and in the nature of their employment. According to the 1926 Population Census, less than half of single women aged 14 or over in the Irish Free State were in employment, compared with over 87 per cent of men. This suggests that there was a substantial level of concealed female unemployment, a phenomenon which probably also existed in rural areas of Northern Ireland, such as Co. Fermanagh. In 1926 one-quarter of women who were described as 'engaged in home duties' were single. Others were classified as unoccupied: the Census would not allow more than one woman in a household of less than seven members to be recorded as 'engaged in home duties'. Although many 'unoccupied' single women were probably fully employed caring for elderly parents or bachelor brothers, it would be naive to assume that they had opted for such

a life-style. The proportion of younger women in paid employment rose gradually and by the mid-'sixties virtually all young
single women were in the labour market.

In 1926 only 5.6 per cent of married women in the Irish Free
State had occupations, compared with 14.5 per cent in Northern
Ireland. Most of these women were either self-employed or
worked in the family economy; there were only 8,000 married
women employees in the Irish Free State in 1926. As the family
economy and self-employment became less significant, so many
jobs which were accessible to married women disappeared. By
1961 three-quarters of women workers were classed as employees,
compared with one-half in 1926. During the 1960s, however, the
economic boom and the loss of women workers through early
marriage resulted in a shortage of women workers in some
occupations, and employers, who had previously operated a
formal or informal marriage bar, began to hire married women,
often on a temporary basis (COMMISSION ON THE STATUS OF
WOMEN). From the 1920s the proportion of widows in the
workforce fell in both parts of Ireland due to improved pensions
and insurance provisions and a decline in the number of young
widows. More recently, however, the rising level of divorce and
marriage break-down, both north and south, has forced a growing
number of women to seek paid employment.

For most married Irishwomen, and indeed for many single
women during this century, work took place in the home: a
combination of child-care, housekeeping and perhaps farm tasks,
plus sewing or knitting for the family. Many women were forced to
eke out modest incomes by making and mending, altering family
clothes to fit successive children and turning flour sacks into
sheets. In ARENSBERG & KIMBALL's sympathetic account of life
on a farm in west Clare in the 1930s, the farmer's wife was first to
rise in the morning and last to retire at night. The same could
probably be said of many urban women. Labour-saving devices
were slow to penetrate Irish homes. Although most families living
in urban areas had access to electricity by the 1940s, most rural
households were only electrified in the following decade and
when electricity was installed families were more likely to buy a
radio rather than any labour-saving devices other than an electric

iron. In 1946 less than one rural household in ten in the Irish Republic had running water on tap and 40 per cent were still without running water in 1971. For women in these households, laundry, family hygiene, even washing the dishes were difficult and time-consuming tasks (DALY 1996). Although Irish households were slow to spend money on appliances such as fridges and washing-machines, the experience in the United States suggests that 'labour-saving' devices did not lead to a reduction in the time spent on housework: housekeeping standards simply rose.[32] Although little is known about changes in Irish housekeeping practices, many women joined groups such as the Irish Countrywomen's Association or attended evening cookery and crafts classes; they also bought many magazines, published in Britain or in Ireland, which catered for women (BOURKE 1993, FERRITER, IRWIN).

(a) *Irish Republic*
   As agriculture became less important in the economy of the Irish Republic the numbers employed fell, though farmers' daughters and sisters disappeared more rapidly than sons and brothers. According to the 1981 Census, only 1,005 daughters and 2,149 other female relatives worked in agriculture. In the 1920s undocumented farmers' wives were the largest group of women engaged in agriculture; this is also true of the 1990s. Employment in domestic service also declined, particularly in the years immediately following the end of World War II when many women opted for better-paid service positions in Britain (COMMISSION ON EMIGRATION). Nevertheless, domestic service employed over 9 per cent of working women as late as 1961. Employment in manufacturing industry rose substantially during the 1930s when women gained 59 per cent of the jobs created in protected industries. Most female employees were young; they worked in unskilled or semi-skilled assembly or packaging tasks in clothing, footwear, toiletries and confectionery plants (DALY 1992). Many of these workers suffered spells of unemployment during World War II due to shortages of raw materials, though employment revived in the immediate post-war years. The 1950s was a decade of economic stagnation; the

number of women engaged in manufacturing in 1961 was virtually identical with 1951. Although the late 1960s and 1970s brought a steady rise in the number of women in industrial employment, their share of the manufacturing workforce fell sharply. By 1981 women held 27 per cent of manufacturing jobs compared with 35 per cent in 1951. This trend was partly reversed during the 1980s.

Service occupations such as clerical work and shop assistance showed long-term expansion. By 1981 one occupied woman in five was a clerk, one in twelve a shop assistant or barmaid (FAHEY). The feminization of clerical jobs began around the turn of the century: by 1911 almost 30 per cent of clerks in the civil service and in private business were women and the number of established female civil servants increased by 140 per cent in the decade after independence (DALY 1995). Women tended to be recruited into low-paid, women-only grades, where they were generally assigned routine tasks. Promotion opportunities were few. Despite these shortcomings, the jobs were hotly contested: although the lowest positions often only required primary school education, many successful candidates had attended secondary school and some men appear to have coveted these jobs. There were widespread complaints during the 'twenties and 'thirties against the employment of so called 'pin-money girls' in white-collar jobs in preference to men (DALY 1979). The growth in white-collar employment from the 1960s brought a rapid expansion of female employment in this sector, though no radical change in the type of work on offer. Women continued to work in sex-specific jobs, performing routine tasks with limited opportunities for promotion.

(b) *Northern Ireland*

Despite the lack of occupational data, it is evident that employment for women in manufacturing industry probably contracted during the 1930s; a decade which was also characterised by high male unemployment. The linen industry suffered a permanent decline during the inter-war years and few new industries emerged. The outbreak of war in 1939 brought no immediate relief. Flax was in scarce supply while the introduction of clothes rationing threatened employment in the clothing sector. In the longer term women transferred into engineering, aircraft manufacture and rope and twine making, and the number of insured women workers showed a modest rise from 111,900 in 1939 to a wartime peak of 118,600 in 1943 (BLAKE). The number of women employed in manufacturing industry fell slightly between 1951 and 1961: employment in traditional textile and clothing industries dropped by almost 20 per cent, though this was partly compensated by growth in other sectors. Although the establishment of new foreign-owned industries in the 'sixties created additional jobs for women, their share of manufacturing employment fell. Since the early 'seventies foreign investment has dried up and both sexes have experienced a dramatic decline in manufacturing employment. By 1981 the number of women employed in manufacturing industry was approximately half the number in 1961, whereas in the Irish Republic the number of women in manufacturing employment showed a marginal increase.

Job losses in manufacturing were more than offset by gains in service employment. The post-war welfare state created numerous jobs for women in health-care and education. Higher disposable incomes led to rising employment in catering and retailing. By 1985 four out of five women were engaged in service employment.

(c) *Women and Trade Unions*
    The history of women's trade union membership reflects women's employment. Domestic servants or women working in agriculture and the family economy were unlikely to join a trade union. Most women members have therefore been drawn from factory workers—particularly Ulster textile workers—or teachers and white-collar workers. As the proportion of female employees has increased, so has the proportion of women belonging to trade unions. The earliest trade unions were founded by men who had served an apprenticeship and sought to protect their privileged status against outsiders, such as unskilled men or women workers who would devalue their skilled status and undercut wages. Most artisans believed that women's place was in the home and used the separate spheres argument to justify demands for a wage which

would enable them to support a wife and family. The first Irish women to join a trade union were members of the INTO, the Irish National Teachers Organisation, which was founded in 1858; from its foundation it recruited women and gave them full voting rights (O'CONNELL). This proved an isolated instance until 1893 when the Textile Operatives Society was founded in Belfast. In 1911 the Irish Women Workers Union was founded in Dublin as the female wing of the Irish Transport and General Workers Union (JONES). Before World War One the small number of women trade union members generally joined all-female unions, though the Drapers' Assistants' Association was a notable exception. After World War One most women joined mixed unions, mainly the general unions, or unions representing workers in teaching, the civil service or local government. Until the 1960s there is no evidence that these unions showed any concern about the fact that women received lower pay or experienced poor promotion opportunities; indeed some union leaders actively condoned legislation which discriminated against working women (DALY 1994). Although a majority of members of the INTO were women, the union reluctantly accepted the imposition of a government ban on married women teachers (O'LEARY), and most trade unions other than the Irish Women Workers Union enthusiastically supported the restrictions on women's industrial employment imposed in the 1936 Conditions of Employment Act (DALY 1992). Even the Irish Women Workers Union was ambivalent about women's rights. Its long-term President, Louie Bennett, saw women working outside the home as a social evil which should be rectified by paying men sufficient wages to maintain a wife and family. Many members held similar views (JONES).

During the 1960s the number of women members affiliated to the Irish Congress of Trade Unions rose from 60,000 to 100,000 and by the late 1970s women and men in the Irish Republic were equally likely to join trade unions (DALY 1994). There was also a sharp rise in the number of women trade union members in Northern Ireland from the 1960s, because the public sector/service jobs which provided a growing number of female jobs were highly unionised (BOYD BLACK). These new members, who were concentrated in white-collar employment, appear to have been more conscious of the lower pay and lack of promotional opportunities for women than women who worked in manufacturing industry. The latter generally worked in jobs which were exclusive to women, whereas women in white-collar occupations often performed similar tasks to men. In the Irish Republic the emergence of more centralised pay bargaining in the 1960s highlighted the gap between male and female earnings. Women trade unionists duly protested and this was a major factor in the government's decision to appoint a COMMISSION ON THE STATUS OF WOMEN (DALY 1994).

(d) *Attitudes Towards Working Women*

The attitudes of trade union leaders and rank-and-file members reflected the views of Irish society concerning women's work. Attitudes in the Irish Free State were extremely hostile to the employment of women, particularly married women outside the home. Although such views reflected Catholic social teaching, they may also have been a reaction to the acute competition which existed for jobs in a society where many young adults were forced to emigrate. The new state imposed a succession of discriminatory measures against working women. From the early 1920s women civil servants were forced to resign on marriage; in 1934 a marriage ban was extended to female national schools teachers. The 1936 Conditions of Employment Act gave the Minister for Industry and Commerce power to ban women from specific areas of industrial employment and to set a gender quota for workers in particular industries. This hostile climate towards working women culminated in article 41.2 of the 1937 Constitution which emphasised a woman's place within the home. Such measures probably hindered the careers of individual women. Talented married women civil servants lost the opportunity to achieve their potential and single women may have been passed over for promotion because of a belief that, in the words of Mary Kettle, they were 'loitering with intent to commit a felony—the felony in this case being marriage';[33] women national teachers who married after 1934 lost their jobs, although the aggregate impact was less significant. Conventions in Ireland and elsewhere at this stage dictated that middle-class women and women in respectable working-class

United States or Britain narrowed considerably in the post-Famine period, largely due to emigration. How far did women share in this process? Given that by the end of the nineteenth century women were more likely to emigrate than men, we should expect that women's wages would also show a substantial increase, though this would not exclude the possibility of a widening wage gap between male and female wages. Ó GRÁDA tentatively suggests that the ratio of male and female agricultural wages was almost identical in 1810 and 1860, with women receiving 55-56 per cent of the male rate, though it had narrowed by 1926-30 when women were earning 67 per cent of the male agricultural wage. Statistics cited by BOURKE (1994) also show that female agricultural wages rose relative to men's between 1890 and 1906. Information for female industrial earnings is equally fragmentary.

Earnings quoted for out-workers in the early twentieth century appear no greater than the sums earned by many domestic spinners in pre-Famine Ireland, though anti-sweating campaigners may have deliberately chosen the worst cases. For the linen industry, the largest employer of women factory workers, data cited by ARMSTRONG suggest that the wages of female spinners and weavers increased relative to the wages of male roughers and sorters between 1860 and 1905. However, EMILY BOYLE argues that until 1914 women's wages rose more slowly than the wages of unskilled men. Reconciling both statements is difficult because of the range of wages quoted and the fact that some relate to piece-work. Women appear to have made some gains relative to men during the 1860s and 1870s, but BOYLE suggests that between the 1880s and 1905 the gap between women's wages and the wages of unskilled men widened. By 1910 adult women were earning 11-12/- (55-60p) per week, about two-thirds the wage of an unskilled male labourer. The gap between male and female wage rates in linen was less than in manufacturing industry as a whole, perhaps because most unskilled male textile workers were in their teens or early twenties. In 1914 unskilled women factory workers earned approximately 56 per cent of the average wages paid to male factory labourers; in Britain the figure was 60 per cent (Ó GRÁDA). The lower relative wages for Irish factory women are consistent with the existence of substantial undocumented female unemployment. The gap between male and female industrial wages may have widened slightly during the 'thirties; in 1939 women in transportable goods industries earned 53 per cent of the average hourly rate paid to men and the ratio was identical in 1960 (DALY 1979). By 1972 it had risen to 57 per cent; in 1980 it stood at 69 per cent, which is similar to the current ratio. These data, which apply to only a minority of male and female workers, overstate the gender gap; in 1987 hourly earnings for all female employees were 80 per cent of the male rate (CALLAN & WREN).

Average earnings for women are lower than those for men in all countries for which data exist. Ireland is no exception, though in the past the gender gap in Ireland appears to have been larger than in other parts of Europe. Lower female earnings cannot simply be attributed to discrimination, though this undoubtedly plays a part. Women workers tend to be younger than men and to have fewer years of experience: in the past this has been particularly true of women employed in Irish manufacturing industry (DALY 1992). Women often work shorter hours. The fact that women have traditionally crowded into a narrow range of occupations meant increased competition for jobs and lower wages; women were less likely to receive training; lack of skill and poor trade union organisation left them with weaker bargaining power(GOLDIN). BLACKWELL attributed the lower pay of Irishwomen to the fact that they were over-represented in poorly-paid occupations. When CALLAN & WREN controlled for variables such as education and experience, they concluded that average female wage rates would be over 10 per cent higher if men and women were remunerated on an equal basis. No single factor appears to explain this differential, though the authors suggest that past discrimination may be one factor. The gap is considerably less than that found by WALSH & WHELAN in 1976. Although the two studies relate to different categories of workers, there are grounds for assuming that legislation on equal pay and anti-discrimination has reduced gender-based differences in wages.

(f) *Recent Developments.*

When the REPORT OF THE COMMISSION ON THE STATUS OF WOMEN examined the profile of working women in the Irish Republic c. 1970 the overwhelming majority worked in occupations which were exclusive to women where promotion prospects were limited and little training was provided. Women workers had low career expectations; most resigned work either on marriage or before the birth of their first child even where no formal marriage ban existed. The publication of this report reflected a rising interest in women's rights, and specifically in working conditions and equal pay. The 1970 Equal Pay Act (Northern Ireland) required employers to give equal terms and conditions of employment to workers employed on 'like work' or 'on work rated as equivalent'. Women in the Irish Republic gained similar protection on 31 December 1975 when the Anti-Discrimination (Pay) Act, 1974 was introduced. The marriage bar which applied to women in public service employment was removed in 1973.

In recent decades both parts of Ireland have experienced a substantial rise in employment among married women. In the Irish Republic the female labour force (employed and unemployed) grew by 54.6 per cent between 1971 and 1992, and the male labour force by only 10.2 per cent. The number of men at work fell by 4.8 per cent, and the number of women at work rose by 40.8 per cent. Although Northern Ireland had a much higher proportion of women in the labour market in 1971, the participation rate of women had also risen by more than one-third by 1991. In the Irish Republic since 1971 the proportion of single women in the labour force has fallen, whereas the proportion of married women had risen from 7.5 percent to 26.9 per cent by 1991. During these years the fertility rate fell from 3.9 to 2.1. Although unemployment among women has increased in both parts of Ireland, women have been more successful than men in obtaining and retaining jobs. However, a growing proportion of women's jobs are in low-paid, often part-time service industries. Thus, the sharp rise in the number of women in paid employment in recent years may reflect changes in the nature of work and the burgeoning demand for a new under-class of workers rather than the benefits of anti-discrimination legislation or growing female assertiveness.

V

CONCLUSION

The history of women's work in Ireland has many features in common with the experience of other countries. In the past women's decisions to undertake paid employment and the types of work which they performed were generally determined by family needs rather than by individual wishes. Until recently most women in the Irish Free State worked within the family economy, often without pay and without being counted by statisticians. Although personal wishes play a much larger role in the work choices made by modern women, the correlation between falling fertility levels and rising employment among married women in the Irish Republic in the past twenty years indicates that demography and wider social issues continue to exert considerable influence over women's work patterns.

Women's work in Ireland must be viewed in the context of declining overall employment in the post-Famine period and the persistence of high levels of emigration. Weak demand for labour constrained women's job opportunities, though emigration enabled some women to opt for better-paid jobs overseas. The weakness of both Irish economies in the post-World War II period accounts for the delayed rise in female occupation rates relative to other countries. When living standards rose in the Irish Republic in the 1960s, the first response of Irish women was, paradoxically, to quit the labour force: poor economic prospects had previously forced couples to postpone marriage or remain single; rising living standards brought a higher marriage rate and earlier marriages. The growing tendency for married women in the Irish Republic to remain in the labour force in recent years may reflect a new materialism within Irish society and changing attitudes towards the role of women. The coincidence between a falling birth-rate and a rising participation rate is particularly striking.

Both parts of Ireland offer contrasting experiences of women in the workforce. In much of Ulster there is a long history of women's factory employment and of married women working outside the home; in the Irish Republic these are relatively recent experiences. Although the lives of women who worked outside the home differed significantly from those who worked within the domestic economy, it is unclear how far this impinged on the wider political sphere. While it seems improbable that the Stormont government would have introduced legislation similar in intent to the Conditions of Employment Act, the share of manufacturing jobs held by women declined in both parts of Ireland from the 1960s, which suggests that while the Dublin government gave overt preference to jobs for men, a similar, more covert process may have occurred in Northern Ireland. There is no evidence that the higher proportion of women in the occupied workforce in Northern Ireland gave rise to a stronger feminist movement or to greater female political representation. For most Irishwomen in the past, work, whether paid or unpaid, was a matter of survival.

NOTES

[1] TILLY AND SCOTT, ch. 5.

[2] FAHEY 1990.

[3] Eurostat, *Community Survey on the Structure of Agricultural Holdings*,1979-80, vol II, p. 201. Census of Distribution 1933, p. 21. See FAHEY 1990, pp. 180-2.

[4] CLARKSON & CRAWFORD 1991, pp. 236-54.

[5] WAKEFIELD, i, 686.

[6] WELD, p. 489.

[7] WAKEFIELD, i, p. 694.

[8] Eric Almquist, 'Mayo and Beyond: Land, Domestic Industry, and Rural Transformation in the Irish West, 1750-1900', Ph. D. Boston University, 1977, pp. 71-2.

[9] Quoted in Almquist, p. 29.

[10] Jean Graham, 'Rural Society in Connacht 1600-1640', in Nicholas Stephens and Robin E. Glasscock (eds.), *Irish Geographical Studies in Honour of E. Estyn Evans* (Belfast 1970). pp 198-199; Charles Mc Glinchey, *The Last of the Name* (Belfast, 1986), p. 27.

[11] DICKSON, 1993, p. 381.

[12] TIGHE, pp. 384-5,387-9,

[13] BOURKE, 1992, p. 103.

[14] WAKEFIELD i, pp. 417, 449.

[15] TIGHE, pp. 179, 195-6, 213; WAKEFIELD, i, p. 464.

[16] POOR INQUIRY 1836, vol. xxxi, App. D.

[17] O'NEILL, p. 103.

[18] Almquist, 'Mayo and Beyond', pp. 253-5.

[19] MAXWELL, pp. 280-1.

[20] POOR INQUIRY 1836, supplement to App. C, part I.

[21] WAKEFIELD, ii, p. 801.

[22] Department of Industry and Commerce, Agricultural Statistics 1847 to 1926, I, 22, p. l.

[23] BROWNE, 1896, p. 99.

[24] SYNGE, 'Erris', p. 325.

[25] James Brenan, 'The Modern Irish Lace Industry'; 'The marketing of Irish Lace' in W.P. Coyne, (ed.), *Ireland: Industrial and Agricultural* (Dublin 1902), pp. 420-435.

[26] BOURKE, 1993, p. 123.

[27] *Committee of Inquiry into the Conditions of Employment in the Linen and other Making-Up Trades in the North of Ireland.* Report and Evidence 1912 (Cd.6509), para. 55; BOURKE, 1993, p. 123.

28 It is impossible to determine the total number of female factory workers; aggregate data in the Census of Production in 1907 does not distinguish between male and female workers.

29 Emily Boyle, 'The Economic Development of the Irish Linen Industry 1820-1913', Ph.D. thesis, Queen's University, Belfast, 1979.

30 Data taken from Peter Flora, Franz Kraus and Winfried Pfenning, *State, Economy and Society in Western Europe, 1815-1975 vol I. The Growth of Mass Democracies and Welfare States* (London, 1983), pp. 553-624.

31 On women in medicine, see J.B. Lyons, *Irish Medical Times*, January 1992. My thanks to Margaret Ó hÓgartaigh for this reference and for information on the 1919 Sex Disqualification Act.

32 Christine Bose, 'Technology and changes in the Division of Labour in the American Home', *Women's Studies International Quarterly*, 2, 1979, pp. 295-304.

33 Commission of Inquiry into the Civil Service, 1932-35, R. 54/2.(Dublin 1935): Addendum C by Mrs. M. Kettle.

BIBLIOGRAPHY

Although the volume of publications concerning Irish women's history has expanded significantly in recent years, much work remains to be done and only a fraction of the research to date has focussed on the question of women's work. However, there is a considerable volume of information on this topic in more general works relating to Irish agriculture, industry, urban history, demography and emigration, which should be consulted. These books and articles are often frustrating: the author's main interest often lay in some other aspect of the question and information relating to women is often fragmentary and tangential. Yet given the scanty nature of the extant material these works cannot be ignored. Reading them also ensures that women's work is placed within the overall context of Irish social and economic history. Material relating to the last twenty years is substantially more plentiful, but as the primary focus of this pamphlet is historical, references to contemporary Ireland have been kept to a minimum.

Many primary printed sources trawled by economic historians can prove productive. Thus, well-known works such as Arthur Young, *A Tour in Ireland*, (Dublin, 1780) or the statistical surveys of Irish counties which were commissioned by the Royal Dublin Society in the early nineteenth century, such as Isaac Weld, *Statistical Survey of County Roscommon* (Dublin, 1830) should not be ignored. Several appendices of the *Poor Inquiry* provide invaluable information about women's work in pre-Famine Ireland, as do the Baseline Reports of the Congested Districts Board. A series of ethnographic studies of the west of Ireland undertaken by the Royal Irish Academy around the turn of the century also contain descriptions of women's work, e.g. Charles R. Browne, 'Notes on the Ethnography of Ballycroy', *Proceedings of the Royal Irish Academy*, third series 1896, vol. 4. Memoirs, autobiographies and photographs provide other useful sources.

Readers of this pamphlet will rapidly realise that statistical data concerning women in the labour market are a mine-field. It is essential, as far as possible, to understand the limitations of sources such as the Census of Population; yet despite the short-comings the Population Census remains an invaluable source. The statistical problems posed by the question of female unemployment are even greater, and for that reason I have virtually ignored the topic.

ALMQUIST, Eric. 'Mayo and Beyond: Land, Domestic Industry and Rural Transformation in the Irish West', Ph.D. Boston University, 1977.

ARENSBERG, Conrad and KIMBALL, Solon T. *Family and Community in Ireland*, (Cambridge Mass. 1965).

ARMSTRONG, D.L. 'Social and Economic Conditions in the Belfast Linen Industry 1850-1900', *Irish Historical Studies*, vii, no. 28 , Sept. 1951. pp. 235-269. A pioneering study.

BARKER, Patricia. 'The True and Fair Sex', in David Rowe, (ed)., *The Irish Chartered Accountant. Centenary Essays 1888-1988* (Dublin 1988), pp. 207-225.

BEALE, Jenny. *Women in Ireland. Voices of Change* (Bloomington, Indiana 1987).

BELL, Jonathan and WATSON, Mervyn. *Irish Farming 1750-1900* (Edinburgh, 1986).

BHREATHACH, Eibhlin. 'Charting New Waters: Women's Experience in Higher Education, 1879-1908', in CULLEN, pp. 55-78.

BIELENBERG, A. *Cork's Industrial Revolution 1780-1880* (Cork 1991),—useful on Cork textile industries.

BLACK, J Boyd H. 'Trade Union Growth and Organisation', in HARRIS, JEFFERSON AND SPENCER, pp. 207-233.

BLACKWELL, John. *Women in the Labour Force* (Dublin 1986). A comprehensive statistical analysis covering the period from the 1960s to the mid-1980s.

BLAKE, John W. *Northern Ireland in the Second World War* (Belfast 1956).

BOSERUP, Ester. *Women's Role in Economic Development* (New York 1970).

BOURKE, Joanna. 'Women and Poultry in Ireland, 1891- 1914', *Irish Historical Studies*, vol. 25, no. 99 1987, pp. 293-310.

————, 'Dairywomen and Affectionate Wives: women in the Irish Dairy Industry', *Agriculture History Review*, xxxviii, pp. 149-165.

————, 'Working Women: the Domestic Labor Market in Rural Ireland, 1890-1914', *Journal of Interdisciplinary History*, xxi, no. 3, 1992, pp. 479-499.

————, "The Best of all Home Rulers': The Economic Power of Women in Ireland', *Irish Economic and Social History*, 18 (1991), pp. 24-37.

————, *Husbandry to Housewifery: Women, Economic Change and Housework in Ireland 1890-1914* (Oxford 1993). An important study of all aspects of women's work in rural Ireland including agriculture, domestic industry and housekeeping.

BOYLE, Elizabeth. *The Irish Flowerers* (Belfast 1971).

BOYLE, Emily. 'The Economic Development of the Irish Linen Industry, 1820-1913', Ph.D. Queen's University Belfast. 1979.

BREEN, Richard. 'Farm Servanthood in Ireland, 1900-1940', *Economic History Review*, 36, 1983, pp. 87-102.

———— & Damian Hannan: 'School and Gender: The Education of Girls in Ireland', in CURTIN, JACKSON AND O'CONNOR, pp. 37-53.

BROPHY, Imelda. 'Women in the Workforce', in David Dickson (ed)., *The Gorgeous Mask. Dublin 1700-1850* (Dublin, 1987), pp. 51-62.

BROWNE, Charles R. 'Notes on the Ethnography of Ballycroy', *Proceedings of the Royal Irish Academy, third series*, 1896, vol. 4. (Other volumes in the period 1896-1906 contain similar studies of life in the west of Ireland).

CALLAN, Tim and WREN, Anne. *Male/Female Wage Differentials: Analysis and Policy Issues.* (Dublin, Economic and Social Research Institute, General Research Series no. 163, 1994).

CARBERY, Mary. *The Farm by Lough Gur* (Cork, 1973 edition) (Life on a large Limerick dairy farm towards the end of the nineteenth century).

Census of Production 1907. Final Report 1912. (cd. 6320). Contains some data on female employment in individual industries but unfortunately no aggregate data on female factory employment.

CLANCY, Paula and MACKEOGH, Kay. 'Gender and Trade Union Participation', in CURTIN, JACKSON AND O'CONNOR, pp. 152-168.

CLARKSON, L.A. 'An Anatomy of an Irish Town: The Economy of Armagh, 1770', *Irish Economic and Social History,* v, 1978, pp. 27-45.

————— & CRAWFORD, E.M. 'Life after Death: Widows in Carrick-on-Suir, 1799', in MacCURTAIN AND O'DOWD pp. 236-254.

—————, 'Love, Labour and Life: Women in Carrick-on-Suir in the Late Eighteenth Century', *Irish Economic and Social History,* xx, 1993, pp. 18-34.

CLEAR, Caitriona. *Nuns in Nineteenth-Century Ireland* (Dublin, 1987).

COHEN, Marliyn. 'Working Conditons and Experiences of Work in the Linen Industry: Tullylish, Co. Down', *Ulster Folklife* 30, 1984, pp. 1-21.

—————, 'Survival Strategies in Female-Headed Households: Linen Workers in Tullylish, County Down, 1901', *Journal of Family History,* vol. 17 no. 3, 1992, pp. 303-318.

COLLINS, Brenda. 'Irish Emigration to Dundee and Paisley during the First Half of the Nineteenth Century', in J.M. Goldstrom and L.A. Clarkson (eds.), *Irish Population, Economy and Society. Essays in Honour of the Late K.H. Connell* (Oxford 1981), pp. 195-212.

————, 'Families in Edwardian Belfast', unpublished paper read to Urban History Conference, Aberdeen 1982.

————, 'Sewing and Social Structure: The Flowerers of Scotland and Ireland', in Rosalind Mitchison and Peter Roebuck (eds.), *Economy and Society in Scotland and Ireland 1500-1939* (Edinburgh, 1988).

————, 'The organisation of Sewing Outwork in Nineteenth-Century Ulster,', in Maxine Berg (ed), *Markets and Manufactures in Early Industrial Europe* (London 1991).

Commission on the Status of Women. Report to the Minister for Finance (Dublin 1972), PR1 2760. Contains chapters on equal pay, employment and women's social welfare entitlement. An invaluable source for the 1960s.

Committee of Inquiry into the Conditions of Employment in the Linen and other Making-Up Trades in the North of Ireland. Report and Evidence. 1912 (Cd. 6509).

COOLAHAN, John. *The ASTI and Post-Primary Education in Ireland, 1909-1984* (Dublin 1984).

CURTIN, Chris, JACKSON, Pauline, O'CONNOR, Barbara. (eds), *Gender in Irish Society* (Galway 1987).

CRAWFORD, W.H. *Domestic Industry in Ireland. The Experience of the Linen Industry* (Dublin 1972).

————, 'Women in the Domestic Linen Industry', in MACCURTAIN AND O'DOWD, pp. 255-264.

CRONIN, Maura. 'Work and Workers in Cork City and County 1800-1900', in Patrick O' Flanagan & Cornelius G. Buttimer (eds), *Cork History and Society. Interdisciplinary Essays on the History of an Irish County* (Dublin 1993) pp. 721-754. Contains an excellent account of women's employment in manufacturing industry in the area.

CULLEN, Mary (ed), *Girls Don't Do Honours* (Dublin, 1987).

————, 'Breadwinners and Providers: Women in the Household Economy of Labouring Families, 1835-6' in LUDDY AND MURPHY, pp. 85-116.

DALY, Mary E. 'Women, Work and Trade Unionism', in MAC CURTAIN AND Ó CORRÁIN, pp. 71-81.

————, 'Women in the Irish Workforce', *Saothar*, 6 (1981), pp. 74-82.

————, *Dublin: the Deposed Capital. A Social and Economic History, 1860-1914* (Cork 1984).

————, *Industrial Development and Irish National Identity, 1922-39* (Dublin 1992).

————, 'Women and Trade Unions', in NEVIN, pp. 99-105.

————, 'Women in the Irish Free State, 1922-39: The Interaction between Economics and Ideology', *Journal of Women's History*, 6 no.4/vol 7 no. 1 (Winter/Spring 1995).

————, ''Turn on the Tap': the State, Irish Women and Running Water', in Mary O'Dowd and Maryann Valiulis (eds), *Engendering Irish History: Essays in Honour of Margaret MacCurtain*, (Dublin 1997).

DICKSON, David. 'No Scythians Here: Women and Marriage in Seventeenth-Century Ireland', in MAC CURTAIN AND O'DOWD, pp. 223-235. Useful material on the elusive topic of farm servanthood.

————, 'Butter Comes to the Market: the Origins of Commercial Dairying in County Cork' in P O'Flanagan and Cornelius Buttimer, *Cork: History and Society*, (Dublin 1993), pp. 367-90.

DINER, Hasia. *Erin's Daughters in America. Irish Immigrant Women* (Baltimore, 1983).

DUGGAN, Carmel. 'Farming Women or Famers' Wives? Women in the Farming Press', in CURTIN, JACKSON AND O'CONNOR, pp. 54-69.

FAHEY, Tony. 'Measuring the Female Labour Supply: Conceptual and Procedural Problems in Irish Official Statistics', *Economic and Social Review* 21, no. 2 Jan 1990, pp 163-191. An excellent discussion of the methodological problems relating to statistical data on the female labour supply in the Irish Republic from 1926.

————, "Housework, the Household Economy and Economic Development in Ireland since the 1920s', *Irish Journal of Sociology*, 11, 1992, pp 42-69.

FERRITER, Diarmaid. *Mothers, Maidens and Myths. A History of the ICA.* (Dublin 1995).

FINLAY, Andrew. 'The Cutting Edge: Derry Shirtmakers', in CURTIN, JACKSON AND O'CONNOR pp. 87-107.

FISCHER, Wolfram. 'Rural Industrialization and Population Change' in *Comparative Studies in Society and History*, xv, no. 2 (March 1973), pp. 158-70.

FITZPATRICK, David. *Irish Emigration, 1801-1921* (Studies in Irish Economic and Social History 1, Dublin 1984).

————, 'The Disappearance of the Irish Agricultural Labourer', *Irish Economic and Social History*, 7,1980, pp. 66-92.

————, 'Irish Farming Families before the First World War', *Comparative Studies in History and Society*, 25, 1980, pp. 339-384.

————, 'The Modernization of the Irish Female', in Patrick O'Flanagan, Paul Ferguson and Kevin Whelan (eds), *Rural Ireland: Modernization and Change 1600-1900'.*(Cork 1987), pp. 162-180.

————, "A Share of the Honeycomb': Education, Emigration and Irishwomen', in Mary Daly and David Dickson (eds), *The Origins of Popular Literacy in Ireland* (Dublin 1990), pp. 167-188.

GOLDIN, Claudia. *Understanding the Gender Gap. An Economic History of American Women* (New York, 1990).

GRAY, Jane. 'Gender and Plebian Culture in Ulster', *Journal of Interdisciplinary History*, xxiv no. 2 (Autumn 1993) pp. 251-70.

GUINNANE, Timothy W. 'The Poor Law and Pensions in Ireland', *Journal of Interdisciplinary History*, xxiv: 2 (Autumn 1993) pp. 271-291.

————, Age at Leaving Home in Rural Ireland, 1901-1911', *Journal of Economic History*, vol 52 (Sept 1992), pp. 651-674. Refutes the belief that farmers' daughters left home at an earlier age than farmers' sons.

HANNAN, Damien and KATSANUONI, Louise. *Traditional Families?* (Dublin 1977); valuable study of modern farming families.

HARRIS, R.I.D. JEFFERSON C.W. and SPENCER J.E. (eds), *The Northern Ireland Economy. A Comparative Study in the Economic Development of a Peripheral Region* (London, 1990).

HEARN, Mona. *Below Stairs: Domestic Service Remembered in Dublin and Beyond, 1880-1922* (Dublin 1993)

HEPBURN, A.C. and COLLINS, B. 'Industrial Society: the Structure of Belfast 1901', in Peter Roebuck, (ed), *Plantation to Partition: Essays in Ulster History in Honour of J.L. Mc Cracken* (Belfast 1981), pp. 210-228.

HEPBURN, A.C. 'Belfast 1871-1911, Work, Class and Religion,', *Irish Economic and Social History*, x 1983, pp. 210-228.

HIGGS, E. 'Women, Occupations and Work in the Nineteenth-Century Censuses', *History Workshop Jnl*, 23 spring 1987, pp. 59-80. Discusses the under-recording of women's employment in the English census.

————, 'Occupational Censuses and the Agricultural Workforce in Victorian England and Wales', *Economic History Review*, xlviii, no. 4, Nov. 1995, pp. 700-16. Higgs suggests that women accounted for over one-quarter of the agricultural labour-force in the years 1851-71, against a published figure of less than 10 per cent.

HILL, Myrtle and POLLOCK, Vivienne. *Images and Experience: Photography of Irish Women, c.1880-1920* (Belfast 1993).

HYNES, Christine. 'A Polite Struggle: the Dublin Seamstresses' campaign, 1869-1872', *Saothar*, xviii 1993, pp. 35-39.

IRWIN, Florence. *The Cookin' Woman. Irish Country Recipes and Others* (London 1949). A cookery book which also contains descriptions of the author's experiences as a travelling cookery instructor in rural Ulster.

IRWIN, Margaret. *Home Working in Ireland. Report of an Inquiry with an Introductory Sketch of the Anti-Sweating Movement* (Belfast 1909).

JEFFERSON, Clifford W. 'The Labour Market', in HARRIS, JEFFERSON AND SPENCER, pp. 148-177.

JONES, Mary. *These Obstreperous Lassies. A History of the Irish Women Workers Union* (Dublin 1988).

KATZMAN, David. *Seven Days a Week. Women and Domestic Service in Industrializing America* (New York 1978).

KEARNS, Kevin C. *Dublin Tenement Life. An Oral History* (Dublin 1994). Informative on women's casual earnings from activities such as dealing.

KELLY, Mary A. 'The Development of Midwifery at the Rotunda 1745-1995', in Alan Browne (ed), *Masters, Midwives and Ladies in Waiting* (Dublin 1995), pp. 77-117.

KENNEDY, Liam. *The Modern Industrialisation of Ireland 1940-1988* (Studies in Irish Economic and Social History, 5, 1989).

—————, *People and Population Change. A Comparative Study of Population Change in Northern Ireland and the Republic of Ireland* (Co-operation North, Dublin & Belfast 1994). An invaluable concise account of trends in population, mortality, marriages, fertility, employment and unemployment since 1911.

KREMER, John & MONTGOMERY, Pamela. (eds), *Women's Working Lives* (Belfast, 1993). Valuable on recent changes in women's employment in Northern Ireland.

LEE, J.J. 'Women and the Church since the Famine', in MAC CURTAIN AND Ó CORRÁIN, pp. 37-45.

LEES, Lynn. *Exiles of Erin: Irish Migrants in Victorian London* (Manchester 1979).

LUDDY, Maria and MURPHY, Cliona (eds)., *Women Surviving: Studies in Irish Women's History in the Nineteenth and Twentieth Centuries* (Dublin 1989).

—————, *Women and Philanthropy in Nineteenth-Century Ireland* (Cambridge 1995).

—————, *Women in Ireland, 1800-1918. A Documentary History* (Cork 1995).

MacCARTER, Geraldine. *Derry's Shirt Tale.* (Derry 1992).

MAC CURTAIN, Margaret and Ó CORRÁIN, Donncha. (eds), *Women in Irish Society* (Dublin 1979).

MAC CURTAIN, Margaret and O'DOWD, Mary. (eds)., *Women in Early Modern Ireland.* (Dublin 1991).

MAXWELL, Constantia. *Dublin under the Georges* (London 1936)

MESSENGER, Betty. *Picking up the Linen Threads* (Austin Texas, 1975). Superb use of oral history to recreate a picture of working life in the Belfast linen mills and factories.

MICKS, W. L. *An Account of the Constitution, Administration and Dissolution of the Congested Districts Board for Ireland from 1891 to 1923* (Dublin 1925).

MINCER, Jacob. 'Intercountry Comparisons of Labor Force Trends and of Related Developments: An Overview.', *Journal of Labor Economics*, 1985, vol 3, no 1 pt.2, S1-S32.

MOKYR, Joel. *Why Ireland Starved. A Quantitative and Analytical History of the Irish Economy, 1800-1850* (London 1983).

MURPHY, Desmond. *Derry, Donegal and Modern Ulster 1790-1921* (Derry 1981)—useful for Derry shirt industry.

NEILL, Margaret. 'Homeworkers in Ulster, 1850-1911', In Janice Holmes & Diane Urquhart (eds), *Coming into the Light. The Work, Politics and Religion of Women in Ulster 1840-1940* (Belfast 1994), pp. 2-32.

NEVIN, Donal. (ed, *Trade Union Century* (Cork 1994).

NOLAN, Janet. *Ourselves Alone. Women's Emigration from Ireland 1885-1920* (Lexington, Kentucky, 1989).

O'CONNELL, T. J. *History of the Irish National Teachers Organisation 1868-1968* (Dublin 1968).

O'CONNOR, Anne. 'The Revolution in Girls' Secondary Education in Ireland, 1860-1910', in CULLEN ed, pp. 31-54.

O'CONNOR, Emmet. *A Labour History of Ireland 1824-1960* (Dublin 1992).

O'DOWD, Anne. *Meitheal: a Study of Co-operative Labour in Rural Ireland* (Dublin 1981).

——————, *Spalpeens and Tattie Hokers: History and Folklore of the Irish Migratory Agricultural Worker in Ireland and Britain* (Dublin, 1991).

Ó GRÁDA, Cormac. *Ireland: A New Economic History 1780-1939* (Oxford 1993). The unsatisfactory index contains no reference to women, but see pp. 218-228 re: fertility and emigration and pp. 238-9 and pp. 248-9 re: trends in female wages.

O'HARA, Patricia. 'What Became of Them? Women in the West of Ireland Labour Force' in CURTIN, JACKSON & O'CONNOR, pp. 70-86.

O'LEARY, Eoin. 'The Irish National Teachers' Organisation and the Marriage Ban for Women National Teachers, 1936-58', *Saothar*, 12, 1987, pp. 47-52.

OLLERENSHAW, Philip. 'Industry', in Liam Kennedy and Philip Ollerenshaw, (eds.), *An Economic History of Ulster 1820-1939* (Manchester 1985), pp. 62-108.

O'NEILL, Kevin. *Family and Farm in Pre-Famine Ireland: the Parish of Killashandra* (Madison, Wisconsin, 1984).

PRESS, Jon. *The Footwear Industry in Ireland 1922-73.* (Dublin 1989).

PYLE, Jean Larson. *The State and Women in the Economy. Lessons from Sex Discrimination in the Republic of Ireland.* (Albany, NY 1990). Discusses the impact of industrial development policy on women's employment in recent decades.

Report of his Majesty's Commissioners for Inquirying into the Condition of the Poorer Classes in Ireland. App. C. Supplement Part I. Queries for parishes in larger towns; App. D Baronial examinations relating to earnings of labourers, cottier tenants and employment of women and children. Supplement. 1836, xxx, (35), (36).

Report of the Commission on Emigration and other Population Problems (Dublin 1954)

SAYERS, Peig. *Peig: the Autobiography of Peig Sayers* (Dublin, 1973).

SCANLAN, Pauline. *The Irish Nurse. A Study of Nursing in Ireland : History and Education 1718-1981* (Manorhamilton, 1991.)

SMITHSON, Annie P. *Myself—and Others.* (Dublin 1944). Interesting insights into the life of a public health nurse in the early years of the present century.

SNELL, Keith. *Annals of the Labouring Poor. Social Change and Agrarian England, 1660-1900* (Cambridge 1985).

SYNGE, J.M. *Collected Works. Vol. II. Prose* edited by Alan Price, (Oxford 1966).

TIGHE, William. *Statistical Observations relative to the County of Kilkenny* (Dublin 1802).

TILLY, Louise A. and SCOTT, Joan W. *Women, Work and Family* (London 1989). A useful introduction to the topic which concentrates on England and France.

TREWSDALE, Janet M. 'Labour Force Characteristics', in HARRIS, JERRERSON & SPENCER, pp. 178-206.

WAKEFIELD, Edward. *An Account of Ireland, Statistical and Political,* 2 vols (London 1812).

WALSH, Brendan M. 'Aspects of Labour Supply and Demand with Special Reference to the Employment of Women in Ireland', *Journal of the Statistical and Social Inquiry Society of Ireland* 22, no. 3, 1970-71, pp. 88-123.

————— & WHELAN, B.J. 'A Micro-Economic Study of Earnings in Ireland', *Economic and Social Review*, 7, 1976, pp. 199-217.

—————, 'Labour Force Participation and the Growth of Women's Employment, Ireland 1971-1991', *Economic and Social Review.* 24 no. 4, July 1993, pp. 369-400.

WARING, Marilyn. *If Women Counted. A New Feminist Economics* (San Francisco 1988). Examines some of the issues arising from the failure to include women's unpaid work in employment and national income statistics.

WELD, Isaac. *Statistical Survey of County Roscommon* (Dublin 1832).

WILLIAMSON, Jeffrey G. 'Economic Convergence: Placing Post-Famine Ireland in Comparative Perspective', *Irish Economic and Social History*, xxi, (1994), pp. 5-27.

YOUNG, Arthur. *A Tour in Ireland* (Dublin 1780).